Know-It-All
FASHION

Know-It-All
FASHION

The 50 Key Modes, Garments & Designers, Each Explained in Under a Minute >

Editor **Rebecca Arnold**

Contributors

Emma McClendon
Katerina Pantelides
Julia Rea
Rebecca Straub
Alison Toplis
Olga Vainshtein

WELLFLEET
PRESS

Brimming with creative inspiration, how-to projects, and useful information to enrich your everyday life, Quarto Knows is a favorite destination for those pursuing their interests and passions. Visit our site and dig deeper with our books into your area of interest: Quarto Creates, Quarto Cooks, Quarto Homes, Quarto Lives, Quarto Drives, Quarto Explores, Quarto Gifts, or Quarto Kids.

10 9 8 7 6 5 4 3 2 1

ISBN: 978-1-57715-174-6

This book was conceived, designed, and produced by

Ivy Press
An imprint of The Quarto Group
The Old Brewery, 6 Blundell Street,
London N7 9BH, UK
T (0)20 7700 6700 F (0)20 7700 8066

Publisher Susan Kelly
Creative Director Michael Whitehead
Editorial Director Tom Kitch
Art Director Wayne Blades
Commissioning Editor Sophie Collins
Senior Project Editor Caroline Earle
Designer Ginny Zeal
Illustrator Nicky Ackland-Snow
Picture Researcher Katie Greenwood
Glossaries Text Alison Toplis

Printed in China

MIX
Paper from responsible sources
FSC® C001701

CONTENTS

INTRODUCTION
Rebecca Arnold

What makes "fashion," rather than just "clothes"?

Is it the way a garment is designed? Or the way it's sold? Or maybe it's the way it's worn? All of these aspects play a part, but the main thing defining fashion is its time-based nature. Built around seasonal shows, the word "fashion" implies a relationship to change and movement. Fashion shapes the type of clothes, accessories, grooming, and even the ways we style ourselves. After all, fashion's second meaning is to shape, to mold, to create something. We fashion ourselves, and in turn, fashion makes us.

How This Book Works

We begin by looking at some of the iconic **Designers** whose work has defined the "silhouette" through the decades, from industry pioneers such as Paul Poiret, Madeleine Vionnet, and Coco Chanel to modern-day trendsetters including Alexander McQueen, Vivienne Westwood, and Marc Jacobs. We then look at the **Themes & Inspirations** behind fashion designers' work, such as the choice of textiles and the influence of movies, sport, and social trends.

But how is fashion created? And where do we find out about it? In **Fashion Cities & Centers**, we look at fashion as an international industry. Although the main designers' collections are shown twice a year in the four most established cities—Paris, London, New York, and Milan—the past twenty years have seen the growth of new locations and fashion centers, for example, Tokyo, São Paulo, and Sydney. As countries such as India and China emerge as sites of both fashion design and media, rather than just production, the industry's global outlook has become ever more important. Fashion cities and countries have also become associated with particular styles; for example, London is often seen as the home of edgy fashions. **The Fashion Calendar** then looks in detail at how the industry is organized around annual "fashion weeks" in these cities and the roles of the various people who arrange and sell the fashion.

From court designers of the eighteenth century to the present day, the fashion silhouette has evolved to reflect the influences of the times.

From Couture to Main Street examines how designers and manufacturers, including Alexander Wang and Prada, produce fashion for different levels of the market—from different types of clothing, such as evening wear or sportswear, to different types of wearers, including businesswomen and teenagers. In each case, specific designers and brands create clothes allied to their own outlook, and in connection with their client base.

Designers and brands then rely on a whole chain of different professionals to enable them to promote and sell their work. **The Media**, from magazines such as *Vogue*, to blogs including Susanna Lau's *Style Bubble*, play a key role in disseminating not only images of new collections and reviews of fashion shows, but also creating a mood and emotional resonance that connects fashion to consumers on a deeper level.

In the late nineteenth and early twentieth centuries, as the fashion industry became increasingly professionalized, new subsidiary industries evolved to support its growth—from advertising to public relations. In the century and a half since then, wider changes such as the emergence of international travel and digital media have spread fashions farther afield, and given more democratic access to fashionable dress.

It is important to remember that it is not only the fashion industry that generates new styles—**Street Style**, the subject of the final chapter, has played a significant role, especially in the way younger people dress. From punk to Japanese Lolitas, it demonstrates the importance of self-fashioning, as well as keeping up with the latest fashions seen on the runway and the red carpet.

Throughout this book you'll find profiles of some of the key names from the fashion industry, including Miuccia Prada, Anna Wintour, Paul Smith, and Bill Cunningham. Each section is broken down into three parts—the **3-second sketch** encapsulates the subject, the main entry delivers the in-depth treatment, and the **3-minute detailing** provides more information about the topic at a glance.

A global industry—the only constant with fashion is that it changes, reinterpreting the past and embracing the future.

DESIGNERS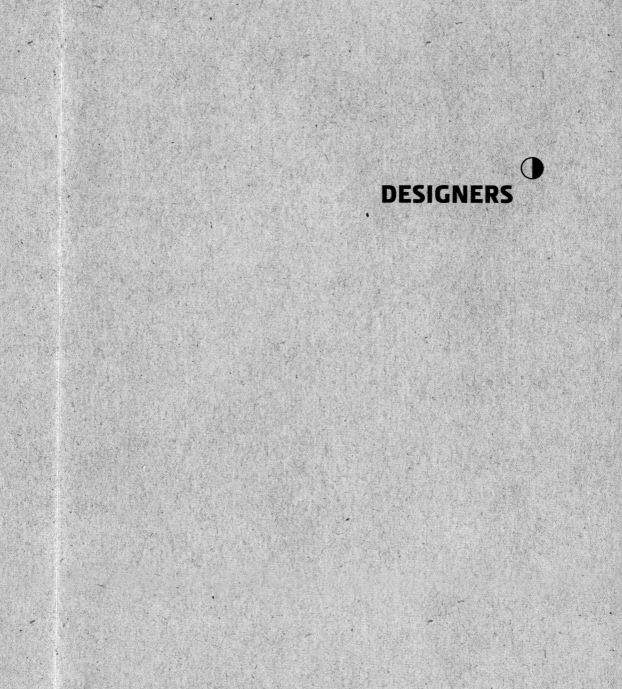

DESIGNERS
GLOSSARY

bias cut Fabric cut on the cross, diagonally across the direction of the weave, which gives the material fluidity and the ability to cling to the body, achieving a close fit.

bouclé wool A woolen fabric with an uneven textured surface of knots and curls, made famous by Chanel with her use of it for her skirt suits.

corset An undergarment that embraces the chest and manipulates the natural waist level, usually boned with steel ribs or, historically, whalebone, to give a structured and supported look to the bodice. Often fastened with lacing and/or hooks and eyes.

Fauvism Fauve is the French word for "beast" and Fauvism was a short-lived (c.1903–08) but influential French art movement characterized by the use of vivid, nonrepresentational color, bold brush strokes, and free treatment of form, exemplified by the work of Matisse.

Futurism An Italian movement that developed around 1909, which rejected traditional forms to embrace the dynamism, movement, speed, and force of modern industrial life. With the focus on the beauty of the machine age and modern technology, the movement remained influential for artists and designers for much of the pre-Second World War period.

haute couture Literally "elite sewing," the haute couture house is based in Paris and is a member of the *Chambre Syndicale de la Haute Couture*. Garments are bespoke, fitted directly to the client, and made by seamstresses from the drawings or ideas of the chief designer before being embellished, for example, with embroidery or beadwork.

Japonisme The first time a significant collection of Japanese objects had been seen in the West was at the International Exhibition, held in London in 1862. This inspired artists of the day such as Whistler and E. W. Godwin, particularly in the decorative arts. Aided by Liberty's, the influential London department store, the movement gathered momentum from the 1870s and had a profound effect on fashion into the twentieth century, particularly Japanese-inspired textiles and kimono shapes.

jersey fabric A material with a knitted appearance that has an elasticity and stretch to it, enabling it both to drape and to cling to the body. Originally made of wool, various fibers, including cotton, silk, and synthetic, are used today in its manufacture.

Orientalist fashion Entirely Western in derivation, the Orientalist takes "Eastern" exoticism, and Oriental embellishments and dress forms, and subsumes them into Western clothing. This can include, for example, richly embroidered textiles, Chinese silks, paisley patterns, saris, kaftans, kimonos, and harem pants, which are then reinterpreted for Western wearers.

pattern cutting The pattern cutter creates the pattern (or template) based on a drawing or a garment that enables it to be further reproduced and look exactly the same. The pattern can then be modified to achieve various sizing and types of fit.

punk A movement that emerged in mid-1970s New York and London. Defiantly antiestablishment and individualistic, it has had an enduring influence, particularly on music and fashion. Originally with a strong DIY ethos, the punk look has since been unfairly stereotyped.

Savile Row A street in London and home to various firms of bespoke tailors, such as Gieves & Hawkes. Now synonymous with the "English gent" look.

silhouette The overall shape that clothes give the body, as if, for example, seen in a black-and-white outline, which helps to determine how the visual aesthetic of fashions change.

Zazou A small dissident subcultural movement in France during the Second World War, typified by their love of garish clothing and swing and jazz music. A tightly rolled umbrella was an essential accessory and oversized jackets were worn in defiance of wartime clothes rationing, when fabric was scarce.

PAUL POIRET

3-SECOND SKETCH

Poiret rejected the corseted silhouette that had dominated Western womenswear since the Renaissance in favor of an Orientalist, holistic conception of the body.

3-MINUTE DETAILING

Poiret regarded his relationship with the women who modeled his clothes as mutually beneficial. He perceived women as orbiting planets, who relied upon his sunlike creativity to shine. However, he also recognized that some women, including his wife Denise and his favorite model Paulette, were true collaborators because they brought his designs to life. This was evident in 1912, when the presence of Poiret's nine models greatly enhanced the success of his European tour.

From his youth, Paul Poiret (1879–1944) had been fascinated with female dress, draping a wooden mannequin that his sisters had given him, in alternately Parisian and Orientalist fashions. When he founded his own haute couture house in 1903, Poiret was inspired by the holistic simplicity of the Japanese kimono, the Classical Greek chiton, and the Middle Eastern kaftan, to relinquish the corset of early 1900s fashion, which divided women's bodies into two distinct masses of bosom and buttocks. He conceived that women's clothing could be supported from the shoulders instead of the waist, and pioneered a draped, rather than tailored silhouette. He also revolutionized women's appearance through his Fauvist color palette of acerbic greens, reds, and yellows, which replaced the pastel tones that womenswear had adopted since the eighteenth century. Poiret's taste for the exotic culminated in the *Arabian Nights*-inspired lampshade-skirted tunics, accessorized with harem pants and a turban, which were worn at his "1002nd Night" party in 1911. His Orientalist aesthetic gained high art status, because it was promoted in the avant-garde illustrations of Georges Lepape and Paul Iribe, and evoked the costume of Sergei Diaghilev's *Ballets Russes*, which arrived in Paris during the same period.

RELATED ENTRIES

See also
PARIS
page 58

MODELS
page 82

HAUTE COUTURE
page 98

3-SECOND BIOGRAPHIES

SERGEI DIAGHILEV
1872–1929
Founder and director of the *Ballets Russes*

PAUL IRIBE
1883–1935
Illustrator whose work for style journals helped promote Poiret's designs

GEORGES LEPAPE
1887–1971
Fashion illustrator who collaborated with Poiret

EXPERT

Katerina Pantelides

Poiret's sinuous, Orientalist silhouettes liberated women from corsets and lent them a relaxed, sensual appearance.

MADELEINE VIONNET

3-SECOND SKETCH
Vionnet's designs
epitomized interwar
fashion—using haute
couture craftspeople to
produce seemingly simple,
fluid designs that were
worn, and copied,
internationally.

3-MINUTE DETAILING
Vionnet's most famous
innovation was her use
of the "bias cut." This
involves cutting fabric
diagonally across the grain
(i.e., on the bias) to make it
springy and mobile—it has
to be hung for a while
before being sewn into
a garment to allow it to
develop its signature
fluidity. In this way,
Vionnet's dresses became
like second skins, adjusting
to the wearer's curves and
moving as she did.

French haute couture reached a peak during the 1920s and 1930s, with female designers dominating. The work of Madeleine Vionnet (1876–1975) stood out for her unique skills in draping fabric directly onto the body to create styles that skimmed the surface of the fashionable modern, athletic physique. She drew upon Classical imagery for inspiration, seeking to reduce dress to its purist form— many designs appear minimal and simple, their intricate cut only visible close up. She honed her aesthetic at various couture houses, Callot Soeurs in particular, where she learned the importance of quality fabrics and the ways these connected with the body when cut with great skill. She did away with corsetry early in the twentieth century—keen to bring cloth and figure into close proximity, and later made special undergarments for her evening dresses, to ensure seams matched and produced the smoothest possible line. During the interwar period, her Paris salon attracted fashionable international clients, who appreciated her references, not just to art history, but also to contemporary art movements, such as Futurism, in her focus on movement and fluidity, and Japonisme in her references to kimonos. She closed her house during the Second World War, but her designs have influenced countless later designers, from Yohji Yamamoto to Calvin Klein.

RELATED ENTRIES
See also
PAUL POIRET
page 14

COCO CHANEL
page 18

TEXTILES
page 36

ART
page 38

PARIS
page 58

3-SECOND BIOGRAPHIES
CALVIN KLEIN
1942–
Sportswear-led designer,
famous for his brand's use
of provocative advertising

YOHJI YAMAMOTO
1943–
Influential fashion designer

EXPERT
Rebecca Arnold

*Drapery and a
monochrome color
palette were key to
Vionnet's designs.*

COCO CHANEL

Gabrielle "Coco" Chanel (1883–1971)

redefined women's fashion through her innovative promotion of simplicity, modernism, and understated elegance. She began her career as a milliner in 1910 and, by 1913, she had expanded her burgeoning fashion empire to include streamlined, luxurious clothing. Rejecting the prevailing corseted silhouette, Chanel's design approach focused upon comfortable, minimalist separates, neutral color palettes, and the innovative use of jersey, a fabric hitherto reserved for men's underwear. She borrowed from contemporary menswear, infusing English tailoring, tweed jackets, and sporty trousers with a newly glamorous appeal as active, modern women joined the workforce. These informal garments were juxtaposed against layers of Baroque-inspired costume jewelry and faux pearls, while a series of instantly identifiable accessories, including two-tone shoes and the quilted chain-handled handbag, promoted a coherent "total Chanel look." Her fusion of luxury with the everyday is evident in the versatile bouclé wool skirt suit: its construction prioritized movement while a gold chain sewn into the hem perfected its weight. From the simple black dress to the sailor-inspired striped top, the garments Chanel popularized remain wardrobe classics, transcending time and trends.

3-SECOND SKETCH

A sartorial shorthand for both classicism and modern glamor, Chanel revolutionized twentieth-century women's fashion by fusing timeless, elegant luxury with everyday functionality.

3-MINUTE DETAILING

Chanel's rare longevity within the fashion industry is encapsulated by her enduring legacy, visible through contemporary main-street imitations and the multi-billion dollar Chanel brand itself. Blending democratic appeal and exclusivity, its aesthetic has morphed with shifting social climates while maintaining a consistent vision. Since 1983, Karl Lagerfeld has balanced the brand's traditions with the necessity of a contemporary reinterpretation, reflecting its heritage while updating it for a new generation.

RELATED ENTRIES

See also
CHRISTIAN DIOR
page 20

PARIS
page 58

HAUTE COUTURE
page 98

3-SECOND BIOGRAPHIES

PAUL POIRET
1879–1944
Designer whose abandonment of the corset preempted Chanel's streamlined aesthetic

CHRISTIAN DIOR
1905–57
Couturier whose restrictive silhouette prompted Chanel to come out of retirement in 1954

KARL LAGERFELD
1933–
Creative Director of Chanel who has reinterpreted the brand's distinctive identity

EXPERT
Julia Rea

A coherent Chanel identity was established through a series of instantly recognizable elements.

CHRISTIAN DIOR

3-SECOND SKETCH
Dior astonished and scandalized the press with his wide sweeping skirts that defied the restrictions of postwar rationing.

3-MINUTE DETAILING
Dior's obsession with silhouette manifested in collections based upon the letters of the alphabet. These included: the H-line in fall 1954, which created an attenuated silhouette by flattening the bosom and elongating the torso; the triangular A-line in spring 1955, which featured small hats and narrow, unpadded shoulders, but widened into a pleated skirt; and the top-heavy Y-line, for fall 1955, which showcased high hats and bulky stoles over sheath dresses.

Christian Dior (1905–57) famously launched what *Harper's Bazaar* editor Carmel Snow termed "the New Look" in 1947. In his "Huit" and "Corolle" models, Dior accentuated the female body's hourglass shape, with diminutive, face-framing hats, unpadded shoulders, defined pointed breasts, a cinched-in waist, mid-calf to ankle-length circle skirts, and spindly, escarpin heels, which gave a hobbling quality to his models' walk. The skirts especially, which used up to 80 feet of fabric, caused a scandal in the press as rationing was still in force. Nevertheless, Dior's classically feminine look, which he claimed "brought back the neglected art of pleasing" after the eccentric and often androgynous "Zazou" fashions of the war years, was in tune with societal and media notions of the return to traditional gender roles in the postwar period. Although Dior exclusively dressed an international elite, his vision of the feminine silhouette filtered into ready-made and home-sewn clothing. Importantly, however, Dior's luxurious new silhouette also promoted the renaissance of Parisian haute couture after its wartime hiatus. Up until his death in 1957, Dior promulgated the idea that dressing was an art, and that the female body was a canvas, which could be refined, embellished, and transformed with each new collection.

RELATED ENTRIES
See also
ANDROGYNY
page 46

PARIS
page 58

HAUTE COUTURE
page 98

READY-TO-WEAR
page 102

3-SECOND BIOGRAPHIES
CARMEL SNOW
1887–1961
Editor of *Harper's Bazaar* who coined the term "New Look"

RAF SIMONS
1968–
Creative Director of Christian Dior 2012–15

EXPERT
Katerina Pantelides

Following the utilitarian austerity of women's wartime dress, Dior's New Look heralded a return to notions of decorative femininity.

CRISTÓBAL BALENCIAGA

3-SECOND SKETCH
Renowned for their technical sophistication, Balenciaga's architectural designs radically altered the relationship between garment and body through their paradoxical blend of fluidity and structure.

3-MINUTE DETAILING
Turning away from the mid-twentieth century's dominant hourglass image of femininity, Balenciaga's bold, streamlined aesthetic formed a backdrop to his experimental innovations in cut, fabric, and texture. His introduction of shortened "bracelet" sleeves and pared-back collars shifted focus from the waist in order to elegantly highlight other parts of the female form, while the invention of staple garments such as the "babydoll" dress and "cocoon" coat produced a universally flattering modern silhouette.

Cristóbal Balenciaga (1895–1972) reshaped the silhouette of mid-twentieth century women's fashion, combining fluidity and purity with a highly sculptural and experimental approach to construction. As a tailor's apprentice in Madrid, he studied couture by copying the designs of Chanel and Vionnet before establishing himself in 1924. Moving to Paris in 1937, he was renowned for his graphic lines, love of texture, and innovative reproportioning of the female form, achieved through fluid drapery and an evolving series of structural shapes. In the postwar years, Balenciaga rejected Dior's waist-defining "New Look," his "barrel line" jackets, which curved upward at the hip, effectively eliminated the waistline. His Spanish heritage was reflected through his heavy use of black, which he often combined with bold shades of red and pink, while dresses with undulating, asymmetrical hemlines echoed the lines of flamenco costumes. In the 1950s, his reinterpretation of the feminine silhouette produced Japanese-inspired kimono sleeves and innovations such as voluminous "balloon" skirts, semifitted suits and tunic dresses. He continued to experiment with volume and proportion into the 1960s, inventing the four-sided cocktail dress in 1967, but his profound disregard for the decade's preoccupation with youth culture was underlined by his sudden retirement in 1968.

RELATED ENTRIES
See also
CHRISTIAN DIOR
page 20

PARIS
page 58

HAUTE COUTURE
page 98

3-SECOND BIOGRAPHIES
CHRISTIAN DIOR
1905–1957
Balenciaga's main rival in Paris from 1947–57

HUBERT DE GIVENCHY
1927–
Couturier mentored by Balenciaga in the early 1950s; his designs displayed a notable Balenciaga influence

NICOLAS GHESQUIÈRE
1971–
Designer who revitalized Balenciaga as Creative Director, 1995–2012

EXPERT
Julia Rea

Balenciaga reshaped fashion's silhouette through his innovative experimentation with volume and proportion.

YVES SAINT LAURENT

Yves Saint Laurent (1936–2008)

first burst into fashion as haute couture's *wunderkind* at the house of Christian Dior. He started there as an assistant at age 19 and took over the helm when he was just 21 years old. After his tenure at Dior abruptly ended, Saint Laurent launched his own haute couture house in 1961. There, he made a name for himself as the *enfant terrible* of French fashion—he put women in trousers, sheer blouses, and gangster-style suits to great uproar. He claimed the street was his most important source of inspiration. This interest led him to open a ready-to-wear boutique in Paris in 1966. Named "Saint Laurent Rive Gauche," the boutique was aimed at the young, fashionable women who populated the student-dominated region of the Seine's Left Bank (Rive Gauche is literally "Left Bank" in French). In later decades, he shed his transgressive reputation to become fashion's great artist-genius known for grand, thematic collections devoted to such topics as the Ballets Russes, Broadway, Picasso, and Opium. Some of Saint Laurent's most distinctive contributions to fashion include his "Le Smoking" women's tuxedo, his safari looks, and his Russian peasant ensembles. Saint Laurent designed for his house until 2002. His eponymous label continues today, and remains one of the most important luxury brands in fashion.

RELATED ENTRIES
See also
CHRISTIAN DIOR
page 20

HAUTE COUTURE
page 98

READY-TO-WEAR
page 102

FRAGRANCES, BEAUTY
LINES & ACCESSORIES
page 108

3-SECOND BIOGRAPHIES
CHRISTIAN DIOR
1905–1957
Couturier whose house Saint Laurent headed from 1957–60

HEDI SLIMANE
1968–
Became Creative Director of Yves Saint Laurent in 2012

EXPERT
Emma McClendon

3-SECOND SKETCH
As fashion's rebel and then as its king, Yves Saint Laurent revolutionized womenswear and became one of the most famous fashion designers in modern history.

3-MINUTE DETAILING
Yves Saint Laurent pioneered the idea of the celebrity designer and became just as famous, if not more so, than the women he dressed. He and his lifelong companion-*cum*-business partner, Pierre Bergé, also set the standard for the modern fashion conglomerate, as we know it today. Together they built a fashion empire on licensing deals, which at one time included everything from cosmetics and fragrances, to luggage and bed linen.

Saint Laurent taught modern women how to dress with his androgynous and fantastical styles.

1969
Born in London to a
working-class Scottish-
English family

1985
Leaves school aged 16 to
apprentice on Savile Row

1992
His entire MA collection
from Central Saint Martins
is bought by fashion
editor Isabella Blow

1996, 1997, 2001
Wins British Designer
of the Year

1996–2001
Works as Chief Designer
at Givenchy

2000
A 51 percent stake in
Alexander McQueen's
own label is sold to the
Gucci Group; Sarah
Burton made Head of
Design for Womenswear

2003
Wins International
Designer of the Year,
awarded by the Council
of Fashion Designers of
America; Awarded A Most
Excellent Commander of
the British Empire (CBE)
by Her Majesty the Queen

2010
Commits suicide in
London. Sarah Burton
becomes Creative
Director of the Alexander
McQueen brand after
his death

ALEXANDER McQUEEN

During his short career,

Lee Alexander McQueen became one of Britain's most globally significant designers. His work combined a sharp eye for tailoring with a cinematic vision that enabled him to create strongly themed collections, which drew on art, film, and history. He designed for strong women, seeking to give wearers power through silhouettes elongated by vertiginously high shoes and dramatic headpieces. Despite this, some misunderstood his collections as demeaning, not realizing the strength he drew from the women around him—including his mother, sisters, and mentor Isabella Blow—and the impact such bold fashions could make, both on the wearer and the viewer.

His early career nurtured his design sensibility—he apprenticed in Savile Row, where he learned about cut and fit in men's suiting, and interned at fashion houses, including Romeo Gigli in Milan, where he gained the ability to work with a rich range of fabrics. These skills were combined with his time at theatrical costumiers Angel and Bermans in London—where he saw how clothes create character and narrative, as well as learning historical pattern cutting. His time as a postgraduate student at Central Saint Martins School of Art and Design enabled him to channel these diverse elements to create coherent collections that expressed his dark aesthetic.

His shows were often controversial; they were steeped in melancholy and influenced by history, most notably "Highland Rape" in 1995, which was inspired by English violence in Scotland during the eighteenth and nineteenth centuries. His shows were also theatrical, using set and styling to evoke mythical worlds. His spring/summer 1999 "No 13" comprised model Shalom Harlow slowly rotating on a wooden platform, as her full, white dress was sprayed with paint by two robotic arms. Other shows drew on Hitchcock films' noirish heroines, created romantic winter tableaux, or saw butterflies released into the audience. Throughout, his emphasis remained on clothing as much as drama and imagery. His innovations included low-slung, tightly cut trousers, dubbed "bumsters," which quickly set a trend in the 1990s, but more significantly, he helped to revive London's status as a fashion city, and constantly drew upon his hometown as a source of inspiration.

He expressed his generation's aesthetic—post-rave, enthralled by punk, disillusioned with accepted notions of beauty, and finding inspiration in art and film. He collaborated with like-minded designers, such as jeweler Shaun Leane and milliner Philip Treacy, always seeking to push fashion design to new limits. His time at French couture house Givenchy was turbulent, as he struggled with its archaic rules and structure, and his best work was for his own label, where he could give his vision full range.

Rebecca Arnold

VIVIENNE WESTWOOD

3-SECOND SKETCH
Rebellious, improvisational, and steeped in British tradition and European art history, Westwood's designs have influenced global fashion style since the late 1970s.

3-MINUTE DETAILING
An early example of a British designer who had international significance, Westwood helped to reinforce London's importance as a fashion capital. She inspired everyone from John Galliano, who rose to fame in the late 1980s, to pioneering Japanese designer, Yohji Yamamoto. Importantly, her work emphasizes fashion's relationship to street style, pop culture, and music, showing its importance within the wider culture. Her interest in history and art makes these connections even more far-reaching.

Vivienne Westwood was at the forefront of punk in the 1970s. Her contribution to fashion spans the DIY aesthetic of those early days, the historically inspired extravagance of the mid-1980s, and more recent forays into ethical design. Lacking formal training, she drew on home-learned dressmaking skills to create the slashed T-shirts decorated with bones, sex shop latex dresses, and tartan bondage trousers that became punk's signature style. Her collaboration with Malcolm McLaren was also present in the ever-changing design of their boutiques. Her later work continued this juxtaposition of tradition with rebellion. Landmark designs include the "Mini Crini" of 1985, which combined 1960s abbreviated styles with the bell-shaped caged petticoats and tight corsetry worn a hundred years earlier. Further collections costumed the wearer as a seventeenth-century goddess or an eighteenth-century gentleman. Her love of traditional fabrics, such as Harris tweeds, is counterbalanced by her use of innovations, including new printing techniques, meaning her work always connects to the present. Her designs continue to propose ways to theatricalize the body, in opposition to what she sees as the ugliness and lack of imagination of mass-produced fashion, which she has criticized for its negative environmental impact.

RELATED ENTRIES
See also
NOSTALGIA
page 50

LONDON
page 56

ETHICAL ISSUES
page 114

PUNK
page 140

3-SECOND BIOGRAPHY
MALCOLM MCLAREN
1946–2010
Multidisciplinary entrepreneur, designer, performer, and manager, his collaborations with Westwood in the 1970s and 1980s fused subculture, fashion, music, art, and performance

EXPERT
Rebecca Arnold

Westwood plays with Establishment ideals, and her work combines both traditional and radical ideas.

MARC JACOBS

Marc Jacobs (1963–) has been a major fashion force since the 1990s. His style unites art, pop culture, sport, and fashion history to create designs that are coveted globally. He is adept at capturing contemporary themes within a single outfit, as evidenced in his infamous "Grunge" collection of 1993 while working for Perry Ellis. The plaid shirts, long skirts, and layered styles were controversial because they brought elements of street style and rock music to the runway. Jacobs continues to use publicity to prompt discussion of his work, developing his persona through interviews and social media, and working with models and photographers who connect intimately with his aesthetic for advertising campaigns—for example, his longtime work with his friend, the film director Sofia Coppola. With hugely popular ranges targeted at varied price points, including, until 2015, Marc by Marc Jacobs, plus fragrance and beauty lines, Jacobs' style is widely disseminated. From 1997 to 2013, he was also Creative Director at French luxury brand Louis Vuitton. He developed its first ready-to-wear line, and revitalized its accessories, most notably through collaborations with artists such as Richard Prince and Takashi Murakami. His work defies hierarchies of high and low art to produce designs that consistently define contemporary fashion.

3-SECOND SKETCH
Marc Jacobs is internationally influential, combining retro and sports inspirations with a love of witty detailing.

3-MINUTE DETAILING
Although sold internationally, Jacobs' most famous retail achievement is his series of stores in New York's West Village. These showcase his anarchic style, spanning his entire range from high-end luxury wear for both men and women to a bazaar-like boutique packed with quirky key rings, purses, and other souvenirs priced at just a few dollars to appeal to younger fans of his brand. The stores demonstrate his ability to design and sell varied products, recognizing his brand's status as an icon of the city.

RELATED ENTRIES
See also
ART
page 38

NEW YORK
page 60

READY-TO-WEAR
page 102

FRAGRANCES, BEAUTY
LINES & ACCESSORIES
page 108

3-SECOND BIOGRAPHY
PERRY ELLIS
1940–86
Designer whose sportswear lines for men and women became popular in the 1970s

EXPERT
Rebecca Arnold

Jacobs' brand encompasses clothes, cosmetics, and everything in between, all imbued with his chic, quirky style.

THEMES & INSPIRATIONS ◐

bias cut Fabric cut on the cross, diagonally across the direction of the weave, which gives the material fluidity and the ability to cling to the body, achieving a close fit.

cheongsam A straight dress with a high collar, the skirt slit on one side, made from cotton or silk and traditionally worn by Chinese and Indonesian women.

crêpe de Chine Originally from China, this is light thin silky fabric, traditionally a mixture of silk and worsted (wool), now manufactured from synthetic fibers too, with the irregular crinkled surface of a crêpe fabric.

drape The way that the fabric falls and covers the body, usually in loose folds.

haute couture Literally "elite sewing," the haute couture house is based in Paris and is a member of the *Chambre Syndicale de la Haute Couture*. Garments are bespoke, fitted directly to the client, and made by seamstresses from the drawings or ideas of the chief designer before being embellished, for example, with embroidery or beadwork.

hip-hop From roots in mid-1970s New York, hip-hop began to reach the mainstream during the 1980s, with its music, a combination of DJs and MCs, and an uncompromising urban street style. Aspirational dressing, in the form of elite sportswear brands and high-end designers, has become a key part of the look.

jersey fabric A material with a knitted appearance that has an elasticity and stretch to it, enabling it to both drape and cling to the body. Originally made of wool, various fibers, including cotton, silk, and synthetic, are used today in its manufacture.

Lycra A synthetic fiber made from polyurethane that brings elasticity and therefore tight fit to clothes, particularly sportswear and underwear. It is woven or knitted in with other fibers, for example, cotton, nylon, or wool, not used alone. Spandex was developed during the Second World War in an attempt to find an alternative to rubber. Lycra was the brand name given to Spandex by DuPont and was commercially manufactured from 1962.

pattern cutting The pattern cutter creates the pattern (or template) based on a drawing or a garment that enables it to be further reproduced and look exactly the same. The pattern can then be modified to achieve various sizing and types of fit.

silhouette The overall shape that clothes give the body, as if, for example, seen in a black-and-white outline, which helps to determine how the visual aesthetic of fashions change.

vintage Generally perceived to be clothing more than twenty years old. As such, clothing will often be secondhand but representative of and immediately recognizable as fashion that originated from a particular decade of the twentieth century.

TEXTILES

3-SECOND SKETCH
The textile is the place where art and science meet to push the boundaries of 2D design and forge 3D fashion.

3-MINUTE DETAILING
A textile altered while already on the runway was Alexander McQueen's spray-painted dress from his spring/summer 1999 collection. A simple white dress with an underskirt of white tulle was spray-painted black and yellow by two robots while worn by a model on a revolving circular platform. The theater of the runway show fused both the futuristic and the artistic elements prevalent in textile design today, and created a seminal moment for McQueen.

The designer's choice of textile, or fabric, is fundamental to how the clothing will turn out. Indeed, the work of some designers has been very much informed by the textile selected. For instance, the draping and clinging properties of jersey have been used prodigiously by designers such as Claire McCardell, Donna Karan, and Azzedine Alaïa. The desired silhouette is achieved through the particular use of specific textiles. Color and pattern, as well as the weight, density, and flexibility of the material all help determine the outcome of a design. Increasingly, textile design is at the cutting edge of technology. Companies such as Jakob Schlaepfer, textile designers for fashion houses including Marc Jacobs, Prada, and Alexander McQueen, work with engineers and scientists to produce innovative, futuristic fabrics that use technology such as optoelectronics. Designers can also visit trade fairs such as Première Vision Fabrics, where textile manufacturers exhibit their collections, working on a cycle 18 months ahead of when the clothes will be shown on the runway. Innovations in textiles have often informed the direction of fashion, from cotton and muslin for the early nineteenth-century neoclassical silhouette, crêpe de Chine for the 1930s bias cut dress, and to Lycra for modern sportswear.

RELATED ENTRIES
See also
ALEXANDER MCQUEEN
page 26

MARC JACOBS
page 30

SPORT
page 44

3-SECOND BIOGRAPHIES
CLAIRE MCCARDELL
1905–58
Designer and pioneer of casual sportswear for women

AZZEDINE ALAÏA
1940–
Designer nicknamed the "King of Cling"

DONNA KARAN
1948–
New York designer famed for creating clothing for professional working women

EXPERT
Alison Toplis

Using a flat piece of cloth, a designer can cling, drape, or create whatever they desire, as mastered by Alaïa in this figure-hugging creation.

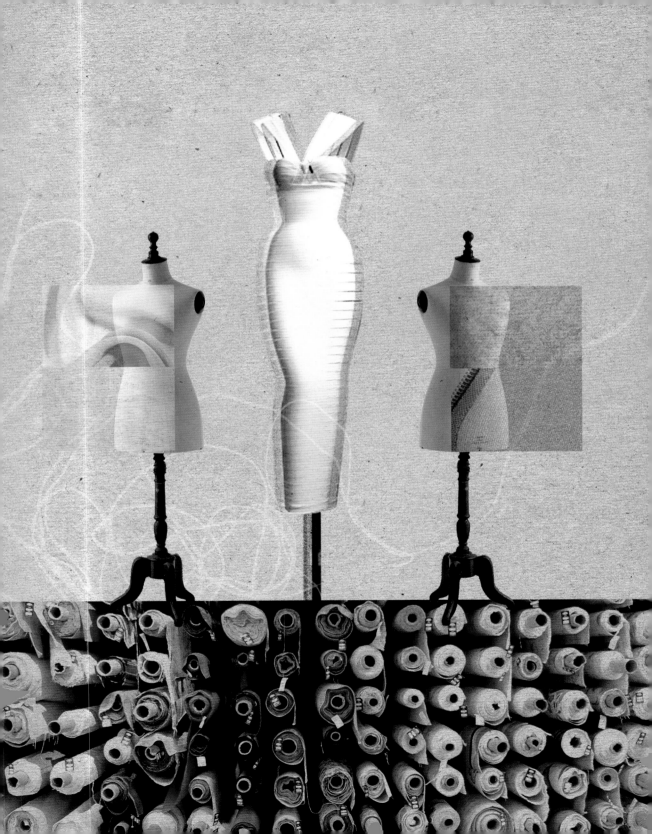

ART

Fashion and visual art are both aesthetic media. Yet fashion's commercialism, mutability, and associations with femininity, are often pitted against the more autonomous, intellectual, and masculine sphere of art. Nevertheless, the fashion and art worlds have continually intersected. Between 1910 and 1930, the artist and designer Sonia Delaunay pursued her signature style of geometric and coloristic abstraction called "simultanism" in the paintings, textiles, and fashions she created. She marketed her dynamic, enveloping "simultaneous dresses" as artworks, rather than transient fashions. Yves Saint Laurent's 1965 shift dresses, which featured the linear color-blocking of Piet Mondrian's paintings, presented a literal transposition of fine art into fashion, as the designer wanted his collection to be imbued with the artist's stark simplicity. During the 1990s and 2000s, Alexander McQueen's and Hussein Chalayan's fashion shows resembled performance art as both designers showed that the design and presentation of clothes could be as subversive as fine art. More recently, several artists have collaborated with major fashion brands. In 2012, for example, Louis Vuitton created a collection with Yayoi Kusama, with the artist's signature bold spot patterns featuring on both the clothes and the in-store decoration.

3-SECOND SKETCH
In recent years big fashion brands have become a presence in the art world through their sponsorship of international art fairs, exhibitions, and museums.

3-MINUTE DETAILING
Is fashion a type of art? Since the 1960s, the art college rather than technical school training of prominent fashion designers has produced diverse collections that express individual creativity, and reinforce the notion that clothing is a form of artistic self-expression. Further, the complex techniques required to make haute couture especially, also denote artistic skill. Additionally, fashion's presence in museums and galleries, spaces originally consecrated to fine art, imbues it with the latter's aura of permanence and gravitas.

RELATED ENTRIES
See also
YVES SAINT LAURENT
page 24

ALEXANDER MCQUEEN
page 26

SHOWS
page 80

3-SECOND BIOGRAPHIES
PIET MONDRIAN
1872–1944
Artist

SONIA DELAUNAY
1885–1971
Artist and designer

YAYOI KUSAMA
1929–
Artist who produced a collection with Louis Vuitton

HUSSEIN CHALAYAN
1970–
Fashion designer

EXPERT
Katerina Pantelides

Saint Laurent's Mondrian dress was a literal expression of fine art's influence on fashion.

1942
Rei Kawakubo born in Tokyo, Japan

1964
Studies arts and literature at Tokyo's Keio University

1967
Becomes a freelance fashion stylist

1969
Begins to develop her own brand, Comme des Garçons

1975
The first Comme des Garçons store, focusing on womenswear, opens in Tokyo

1978
Comme des Garçons adds a menswear line

1981
Comme des Garçons exhibits at Paris fashion week, and the collection astounds critics owing to its antifashion austerity

1984
Kawakubo's protégé Junya Watanabe graduates from the Bunka Fashion College and undertakes a pattern-cutting apprenticeship at Comme des Garçons, and will continue to design for the brand in subsequent years

Early 1990s
Kawakubo launches the magazine *Six*, named after the sixth sense, to document and publish her inspirations

2008
Kawakubo successfully collaborates with the Swedish retailer H&M to create a lower-cost diffusion line

REI KAWAKUBO

Rei Kawakubo received no formal training in fashion design. Nevertheless, her sense of how women's clothes, especially, should appear and feel, developed during her work as a stylist in the late 1960s. Kawakubo claims that she chose the French name Comme des Garçons, which translates as "like the boys," for her brand, simply because she liked the way it sounded. Still, this coincidental, androgynous reference supports Kawakubo's belief that "fashion design is not about revealing or accentuating a woman's body; its purpose is to allow a person to be what they are." Thus, Kawakubo's designs challenge conventional notions of feminine attractiveness, which require women to conform to a patriarchal ideal. Rather than highlighting the body's curves through close fit and high finish, Kawakubo's garments often move independently from the body and proudly reveal their construction. Although Comme des Garçons has traditionally employed a monochrome palette of blacks, whites, and grays, the garments' luxury derives from a use of rare, natural fabrics, some of which come from specialist Japanese weavers.

When Comme des Garçons debuted in Paris in 1981, the monochrome collection markedly contrasted with the ostentatiously luxurious French designers' outputs, and was insensitively dubbed by some critics as "Hiroshima chic,"

after the bomb that devastated the Japanese city in 1945. During the course of the 1980s however, Kawakubo's alternatives to Western excess, which included skirts with jacket sleeves and pants with sweat cuffs, gained critical acclaim for their inventiveness. Indeed, Kawakubo took pride in her clothes' innovation, claiming that she endeavored "to make clothes that are new, that didn't exist before, and hope that people get energy and feel positive when they wear them." Taking a conceptual approach to fashion, she uses clothing to express ideas. For example, a spring/summer 2012 collection, which showcased models cocooned in bridal white and lace textures, delicately parodied the excessive expectations placed upon marriage. However, like her fellow Japanese designer Yohji Yamamoto, Kawakubo disapproves of fast fashion cycles, which cause the previous season's collection to appear dated, and thus also seeks to create unfashionable clothes with integrity, that will wear well over time.

Despite her singularity, Kawakubo has been remarkably open to collaborations with other designers, including Azzedine Alaïa and Vivienne Westwood, and in 2008 with the Swedish main-street retailer H&M. This openness implies that Kawakubo intends that her unique approach to clothing and style should reach an ever-growing audience.

Katerina Pantelides

MOVIES

As well as defining a character's personality and status, movie costume creates narrative and emotional resonance. For the audience, costume helps to construct the movie's milieu and aesthetic. From its earliest days, movies have been an ideal medium to display fashions, and inevitably, to affect fashion itself. Hollywood dominated from the 1920s, with chain stores selling movie-star-inspired styles to eager fans. As color film stock emerged, fashion shows also became a favored plot device in movies such as *The Women* (1939) as a way of displaying glamorous designs and allowing the audience to dream. Costume designers helped to create the stars' style—Joan Crawford was known for wearing the big-shouldered suits designed by Adrian. Fashion designers also lent their skills to big productions, keen to project their work to a captive audience, Givenchy's costumes for Audrey Hepburn being a prime example. Such collaborations underline the interconnections between fashion and movies, with magazines still referencing Hepburn's iconic look from *Breakfast at Tiffany's* (1961). More recently, fashion brands have recognized the movie's power to espouse their seasonal message—with digital media providing an ideal platform to disseminate short, arty films to a huge audience, for example, Autumn de Wilde's witty series for Prada in 2015.

3-SECOND SKETCH
Movies bring style to a global audience, from long leather coats in *The Matrix* (1999) to cheongsams in *In The Mood for Love* (2000).

3-MINUTE DETAILING
Movie costume instantly transports the viewer to another time and place. Historical styles, such as Milena Canonero's designs for *Marie Antoinette* (2006) inspired soft pastels and rococo frills in fashion magazines. Equally, movie stars are important assets to fashion brands, with actors fronting advertising campaigns, and the red carpet becoming a runway show displaying the latest styles.

RELATED ENTRIES
See also
NOSTALGIA
page 50

MIUCCIA PRADA
page 64

3-SECOND BIOGRAPHIES
EDITH HEAD
1897–1981
Dominated Hollywood design for decades, including designing costumes for many of Alfred Hitchcock's movies

ADRIAN ADOLPH GREENBERG
1903–59
Known simply as "Adrian," his hugely successful work on mid-twentieth-century Hollywood movies led to his own fashion line

MILENA CANONERO
1946–
Costume designer whose work is based on meticulous research and attention to detail

EXPERT
Rebecca Arnold

Iconic movie costumes translate into mainstream fashions, and provide inspirations for millions of viewers.

SPORT

3-SECOND SKETCH
From sneakers to hoodies, sportswear-inspired fashion dominates the way people dress globally.

3-MINUTE DETAILING
Sportswear brands' collaborations with fashion designers underline the symbiotic relationship between the two genres. Japanese brand Sacai's designs for Nike unite high fashion with sportswear, and bring street style credibility and a larger audience to the designer. Smaller, one-off collaborations include Adidas' with Brazilian label The Farm Company, which used the latter's signature bright prints to create a vibrant reinvention of Adidas' famous triple stripe designs.

From sportswear giants including Australia's Rip Curl, America's Nike, and Germany's Adidas to niche brands such as Japanese label A Bathing Ape, sportswear dominates contemporary fashion. As dress codes gradually became more relaxed in the late twentieth century, sportswear infiltrated everyday wardrobes. In addition, sportswear is one of high fashion's major references in recent years; for example, Alexander Wang's 2015 collections used sneaker detailing as a decorative element on clingy dresses. Sports stars have long been fashion influencers—in the 1920s, French tennis player Suzanne Lenglen sparked a trend for shorter skirts, while more recently footballer David Beckham has featured heavily in men's style magazines, inspiring multiple grooming and style trends. From the 1930s, sport stars have fronted clothing ranges and given visibility to the fit, athletic physique that has dominated since then. Sport's influence is therefore doubly significant—affecting not just the way people dress, but also the way they think about their bodies. While America is known for having the most sportswear-inspired fashion designers—tarting with Claire McCardell in the 1930s—it is also home to hip-hop, whose stars from Snoop Dogg to Pharell Williams have ensured sportswear remains globally significant.

RELATED ENTRIES
See also
COLLABORATIONS
page 112

HIP-HOP
page 146

3-SECOND BIOGRAPHIES
JEAN RENÉ LACOSTE
1904–96
Tennis player, who turned his nickname "the crocodile" into a logo that is still used by the Lacoste brand

CLAIRE MCCARDELL
1905–58
Designer, whose relaxed yet smart, sporty styles crystallized New York's fashion style in the 1930s

PHILIP HAMPSON KNIGHT
1938–
In 1964, he cofounded the sportswear label that would become Nike Inc., one of the world's most influential brands

EXPERT
Rebecca Arnold

From active sportswear to high fashion—sport is one of the biggest influences on what we wear every day.

ANDROGYNY

Androgyny is one of fashion's most persistent recurring themes and aesthetics, with its potent collision of traditional ideas of masculinity and femininity constructing an entirely separate aesthetic founded on modernity and ambiguity. The flapper girls of the 1920s are widely considered to be sartorial androgyny's first and most visible advocates, promoting flattened breasts, eradicated waistlines, and short cropped hair as a decade-defining ideal of beauty and sexuality. This boyish silhouette coincided with young women being afforded new social and sexual freedoms. The 1930s saw Coco Chanel eroticize and legitimize menswear elements such as tailoring and pants as sartorial symbols of feminine power and strength. Androgyny's reemergence in the 1960s and 70s was similarly catalyzed by the influence of feminism and the sexual liberation movement. Yves Saint Laurent lent femininity a modern appeal with the iconic "Le Smoking" tuxedo suit of 1966. Musicians such as Marc Bolan and Mick Jagger glamorized the feminization of menswear with their long hair, makeup, and layers of jewelry. Fashion's acknowledgment of the increasing fluidity of gender definitions has extended to the twenty-first-century runway, reflected through the use of transgender and gender ambiguous models.

3-SECOND SKETCH
A powerful fusion of masculinity and femininity, androgyny reverses, subverts, and eradicates stereotypical gender-specific aesthetic boundaries in order to express identity, sexuality, beauty, and modernity.

3-MINUTE DETAILING
The late twentieth and early twenty-first centuries have seen androgyny return to the fore of mainstream fashion, with designers challenging traditional gender roles and stereotypes. In 1985, designer Jean Paul Gaultier playfully subverted and erased existing boundaries by creating skirts for men, while the minimalistic aesthetic of the 1990s provided a backdrop to the unisex approach of designers such as Helmut Lang, Comme des Garçons, and Calvin Klein.

RELATED ENTRIES
See also
YVES SAINT LAURENT
page 24

EROTICISM
page 48

MODELS
page 82

MENSWEAR
page 104

3-SECOND BIOGRAPHIES
MARLENE DIETRICH
1901–92
Actress whose eroticized interpretations of menswear in the 1930 movies *Morocco* and *The Blue Angel* sparked controversy

YVES SAINT LAURENT
1936–2008
Designer who revolutionized women's fashion with the "Le Smoking" tuxedo trouser suit

EXPERT
Julia Rea

From flappers and movie stars to rockers such as Marc Bolan, fashion's relationship with androgyny is both enduring and complex.

EROTICISM

RELATED ENTRIES
See also
ANDROGYNY
page 46

EDITORIAL
page 122

ADVERTISING
page 124

3-SECOND SKETCH

Echoing fashion's potential for seduction and pleasure, eroticism is employed to project fantasies that promote or subvert contemporary ideals of desirability and suggest uninhibited alternative identities.

3-MINUTE DETAILING

The notion of fashion's "shifting erogenous zones," a phrase coined by dress historian James Laver, is deeply rooted in both clothing's close proximity to the body and changing and often culturally-specific ideals of the female form. From Vionnet's 1930s backless dresses to McQueen's influential low-slung 1996 "bumster" pants, fashion's conscious emphasis of specific body regions continually creates new sartorial and visual sites of fantasy and eroticism.

Fashion's preoccupation with eroticism is unsurprising given its overlaps with the qualities central to the very nature of fashion itself: desire, pleasure, seduction, and powerful visual appeal. Close links to self-image and identity inevitably transforms fashion into a vehicle for sexual expression, while the tactile appeal of clothing being worn directly against the skin possesses a more explicit erotic potential. The aspirational value embedded in certain fashion objects can also possess a near-fetishistic quality akin to sexual desire, with consumers seeking validation and gratification through the acquiring of desirable products. Similarly, designers and photographers look to eroticize elements in order to communicate their visions of fashion and femininity, whether amplifying and objectifying the female form, or subverting traditional notions of sexuality. The *femme fatale* aesthetic of Hedi Slimane's designs for Saint Laurent, for example—all thigh-grazing leather, ripped, sheer fabric, and navel-grazing necklines—recalls the dark glamor of fashion photographers Guy Bourdin and Helmut Newton, both grounded in a hedonistic vision of assertive 1970s erotica. Conversely, Jean Paul Gaultier's hyper-camp corseted showgirls, sequin-clad sailors, and bondage-inspired lingerie plays with the stereotypes and mutability of erotic identity.

3-SECOND BIOGRAPHIES

AZZEDINE ALAÏA
1940–
Designer whose figure-hugging sheath dresses underpinned the erotically assertive aesthetic of the 1980s

JEAN PAUL GAULTIER
1952–
Designer whose playful subversion of sexuality and eroticism is visible through his championing of underwear-as-outerwear, in particular his iconic cone-breasted corsets

EXPERT
Julia Rea

Fashion both amplifies and subverts ideas of eroticism to create fantasy and meaning.

NOSTALGIA

3-SECOND SKETCH

Fashion's relationship with nostalgia is complex and contradictory, presenting an interplay between past and present that simultaneously romanticizes and reinterprets the past while maintaining its desire for the new.

3-MINUTE DETAILING

The cultural tendency to fetishize the past is visible through the vogue for secondhand or vintage clothing, which accelerated during the 1980s. Rejecting high fashion's often stylized and artificial recycling of historical elements, this type of clothing is often employed as a means of authentic sartorial self-expression, as well as providing an affordable alternative to commercial fashions.

The fashion industry is defined by its preoccupation with "the new" and its fundamentally ephemeral nature yet, paradoxically, it continually looks to the past for inspiration and validation. As with art, music, and movies, fashion's relationship with nostalgia has gained a renewed momentum in the twenty-first century. In an era characterized by fast-paced technology and cultural sanitization, designers have increasingly been drawn to nostalgic aesthetics in order to recreate the sensation of "the new" and reconstruct a romanticized vision of a past rich in meaning, narrative, and authenticity. The designs and advertising imagery of Miuccia Prada and Marc Jacobs, for example, are often filtered through a lens of nostalgia, harking back to lost ideals of glamor and recalling the styles of previous decades in order to infuse both the designs and brand identity with authenticity, while avoiding overtly reverential reproduction by updating these aesthetics with touches of modernity. Wholly new and innovative ideas have become a rarity within fashion design, with historical elements continually being revived and blended together in order to create fresh interpretations and new relevance, whether offering a rose-tinted perspective on a lost, idealized age or becoming tinged with a sense of irony.

RELATED ENTRIES

See also
MARC JACOBS
page 30

MOVIES
page 42

MIUCCIA PRADA
page 64

3-SECOND BIOGRAPHIES

CHRISTIAN DIOR
1905–57
Couturier whose signature hourglass silhouette of 1947 displayed a nostalgia for prewar notions of femininity

MARC JACOBS
1963–
Designer whose designs and dreamlike advertising imagery create a soft-focus vision of femininity grounded in nostalgic influences

EXPERT

Julia Rea

Past fashions are continually revived and reinterpreted by designers, blending nostalgia with a modern perspective.

FASHION CITIES & CENTERS

costume jewelry Traditionally, this is jewelry made with imitation gemstones and not using precious metals. It is worn to embellish a specific outfit at an affordable price. Coco Chanel and Hollywood movies from the 1930s to the 1950s were particularly influential in spreading the popularity of costume jewelry. Today it can be highly sought after, and costume jewelry designed by couturiers or well-known jewelry designers can command high-end prices.

fashion capital A world city that is both a site for the production and the display of fashion, and where the fashion culture of that city is unique and immediately identifiable as being from that locality. This fashion culture is vitally important to that city in terms of cultural and economic output, and their emanating style innovations will influence general global fashion trends.

gamine A woman who is typically slim, mischievous, often childlike, and somewhat boyish, perhaps with cropped hair, sums up the gamine style.

haute couture Literally "elite sewing," the haute couture house is based in Paris and is a member of the *Chambre Syndicale de la Haute Couture*. Garments are bespoke, fitted directly to the client, and made by seamstresses from the drawings or ideas of the chief designer before being embellished, for example, with embroidery or beadwork.

hip-hop From roots in mid-1970s New York, hip-hop began to reach the mainstream during the 1980s, with its music, a combination of DJs and MCs, and an uncompromising urban street style. Aspirational dressing, in the form of elite sportswear brands and high-end designers, has become a key part of the look.

lengha (also known as *lehenga* or *ghagra*) A long, embroidered, and pleated skirt from South Asia worn with a choli, a midriff-baring tight blouse, and a dupatta, a shawl or scarf.

punk A movement that emerged in mid-1970s New York and London. Defiantly antiestablishment and individualistic, it has had an enduring influence, particularly on music and fashion. Originally with a strong DIY ethos, the punk look has since been unfairly stereotyped.

ready-to-wear Clothing that is mass-manufactured in standard sizes and bought by a consumer without prefitting or individual preordering—that is the majority of clothing bought by consumers today.

sari A garment traditionally worn by South Asian women, consisting of a long rectangle of fabric, one end wrapped around the waist to form a full-length skirt, the other end draped over the shoulder or head.

Savile Row A street in London and home to various firms of bespoke tailors, such as Gieves & Hawkes. Now synonymous with the "English gent" look.

sherwani A formal knee-length coat, traditionally worn by South Asian men, which buttons up to the neck and has a small stand-up collar.

street style Fashion innovations or trends that come from, for example, music or subcultural arenas, that is the "street," rather than from fashion designers. These may then influence elite and mainstream fashion, for instance, the black leather motorcycle jacket.

sweatshop A factory or workshop where manual workers are employed for long hours with low pay and under poor or dangerous conditions, with very few workers' rights. Local laws may also have been violated, for instance, the use of child labor or disregarding minimum wage pay levels, with workers exploited to produce cheap goods for manufacturers, usually to sell to the West.

LONDON

While Savile Row's tailors set international standards for menswear throughout the nineteenth and early twentieth centuries, London did not become a fashion destination for womenswear until the 1960s, when designers such as Mary Quant and Barbara Hulanicki created free-flowing, irreverent clothes for the generation of postwar baby boomers, who rejected the 1950s stiff, fussy, Paris-imitation garments. These designers' supremely young aesthetic was promoted by unpolished, gamine models, such as Jean Shrimpton and Twiggy, and the haphazard, cluttered atmosphere of their boutiques resembled thrift stores rather than Parisian couture houses. Theatricality and eccentricity have remained staples of London fashion. For the past five decades, the close association between an art-school education and fashion design have encouraged creative self-expression, sometimes at the expense of commercialism. Nevertheless, the innovative, sometimes provocative work of fashion design graduates at top London art schools has gained international recognition. Subsequently, London schools have nurtured leading international talents, including Mary Katrantzou and Erdem Moralioglu, and graduates have attained prominent positions at global fashion brands.

RELATED ENTRIES
See also
ART
page 38

MODELS
page 82

SAVILE ROW
page 100

3-SECOND BIOGRAPHIES
MARY QUANT
1934–
Fashion designer who was a key figure in 1960s' London youth fashion

BARBARA HULANICKI
1936–
Fashion designer who opened the Biba boutique in London in 1964

MARY KATRANTZOU
1983–
Fashion designer who studied at Central Saint Martins and based her label in London

EXPERT
Katerina Pantelides

London gained a reputation for youth fashion in the 1960s, and is still associated with sartorial innovation.

3-SECOND SKETCH
London fashion's eclecticism extends to its consumers, who subvert traditional boundaries of formal and casualwear, vintage and modern clothing, to create and document their personal style.

3-MINUTE DETAILING
Writers including Robert O'Byrne have argued that elite fashion's growth in London has been challenged by the long-held British prejudice that fashion is frivolous, transient, and not worth investing in. Instead, consumers' desires for low-cost sartorial novelty have been met by main-street chains, which have achieved international recognition in their own right. This is especially true of Topshop, a trend-conscious, ready-to-wear brand.

PARIS

RELATED ENTRIES
See also
COCO CHANEL
page 18

CHRISTIAN DIOR
page 20

HAUTE COUTURE
page 98

The French capital's association

with the latest fashions dates back to the seventeenth-century court of Louis XIV at Versailles. From the opening of Charles Frederick Worth's couture house in 1858, which adapted ornately preconceived designs for elite women and therefore posited a feminine ideal, female dress gained the status of an art form in the city. During the early to mid twentieth-century, Paris-based couturiers, such as Coco Chanel and Christian Dior, were typically French. However, from the mid-1970s onward, overseas designers, including Issey Miyake and Azzedine Alaïa, were invited to showcase their collections in Paris. This, along with the prominence of renowned and talented international designers at the head of Parisian fashion houses (for example, British Clare Waight Keller at Chloé or Belgian Raf Simons at Christian Dior), has given Paris the status of a visionary, global fashion capital. However, the city's female inhabitants, *parisiennes*, continue to be mythologized as ideal consumers, because they have the reputation for seamlessly incorporating current trends into their personal style without becoming fashion victims. Indeed, the mythic *parisienne*, defined by her consciously carefree approach to fashion, is a prominent figure in international fashion editorials and advertisements.

3-SECOND SKETCH
Perhaps the most iconic fashion capital of all, Paris is the birthplace of haute couture.

3-MINUTE DETAILING
The global financial crisis of 2008 led to the promotion of understated simplicity above spectacle in both Paris-based designer collections, and *parisiennes*' personal style. For example, Isabel Marant, who emphasizes practicality and versatility in her reversible jackets and tops that can be worn as dresses, has enjoyed great popularity since 2010. Similarly, Emmanuelle Alt, Editor of French *Vogue*, has stressed the mood for earthy, identifiable figures in fashion editorials, rather than extravagant escapism.

3-SECOND BIOGRAPHIES
CHARLES FREDERICK WORTH
1825–95
Designer, considered the father of haute couture

ISABEL MARANT
1967–
Designer who specializes in high-quality ready-to-wear

RAF SIMONS
1968–
Creative Director at Christian Dior 2012–15

CLARE WAIGHT KELLER
1970–
Creative Director at Chloé

EXPERT
Katerina Pantelides

Paris's architecture has provided a perennial backdrop for fashion photographers.

NEW YORK

New York's fashion industry is as modern as its architecture. Built on ready-to-wear, rather than couture, it has the reputation for being democratic and new—as opposed to "Old World," elite dress, as epitomized by Paris. That said, it took until the mid-twentieth century to shake the idea that all New York fashion did was reproduce trends pioneered by the French capital. It really came into its own during the Second World War, when it cemented its place as the center of sports-inspired fashions. Seventh Avenue emerged in the early twentieth century as the core of the American fashion system—mass-producing fashions at all price points. Allied to this, by the 1930s, was a push to define its own style that could be publicized to domestic and international audiences. Designers such as Claire McCardell crystallized the city's "look"—interchangeable separates, sporty, athletic styles, and the notion of a customer that was active and busy, who needed easily adaptable clothes. This style continued, made glamorous and decadent by Halston in the 1970s, and becoming internationally dominant with Donna Karan, Calvin Klein, and Ralph Lauren a decade later. New York's street style is equally vibrant, from punk to hip-hop, but the city's fashion signature has remained more focused on commercial styles.

3-SECOND SKETCH
New York Fashion Week is the hub of commercial fashion, attracting international designers who benefit from its slick PR machine.

3-MINUTE DETAILING
New York has had a creative revival in the 2000s, with younger designers, from Rodarte to Alexander Wang, Jason Wu, and Prabal Gurung bringing more diversity—both in terms of the designers' ethnicity and the types of designs offered. This has been accompanied by a rise in influential menswear designers, such as Thom Browne, whose womenswear has also shown the city's more nostalgic and theatrical side.

RELATED ENTRIES
See also
SPORT
page 44

READY-TO-WEAR
page 102

PUNK
page 140

HIP-HOP
page 146

3-SECOND BIOGRAPHIES
ELEANOR LAMBERT
1903–2003
Public relations pioneer and a major influence on the development of the American fashion industry

DIANE VON FURSTENBERG
1946–
Fashion designer, most famous as creator of the "wrap dress" in 1974; President of the Council of Fashion Designers of America (CDFA) since 2006

EXPERT
Rebecca Arnold

Driven by a sassy, commercial style, New York fashions reflect the city's dynamism.

MILAN

Standing alongside London, Paris, and New York as one of the four principal global fashion capitals, Milan came to the fore as a hub of Italian fashion design and manufacturing in the 1970s. The city drew upon its close proximity to textile manufacturers, strong infrastructure, and rich history as a site of industrial design to become an internationally recognized epicenter of the fashion industry. Its success was influenced by developments in ready-to-wear clothing, which the Italian fashion industry embraced as a lucrative and accessible alternative to couture for the era's new youth-driven market. The first veritable ready-to-wear fashion show was held in Milan in 1972, featuring textile companies such as Missoni, which reflected the city's propensity for innovative production techniques and its position at the heart of the country's industrial landscape. As the nucleus of Italy's fashion press and advertising industries, brands such as Versace, Prada, and Gucci saw Milan as a logical base for their businesses and in 1978, the "Milano Collezioni," the earliest form of the Milan Fashion Week shows, was established. Uniting fashion and industry, Milan became renowned for its spectacular shows, glamorous aesthetic, and its blending of traditional craftsmanship and innovative technology in the creation of luxury leather goods and textiles.

3-SECOND SKETCH

The epicenter of the Italian fashion industry, Milan is one of four principal global fashion capitals, distinguished by its emphasis on luxury goods and glamor.

3-MINUTE DETAILING

In the twenty-first century, Milan's influence as a fashion center extends beyond its starring role in the biannual international fashion show calendar. With its near-mythical connotations of unparalleled glamor and glossily packaged aspiration, Milan has become a year-round destination for fashion "tourism," drawing legions of international consumers to its high-end shopping opportunities. Simultaneously, the city has become a global symbol of luxury, taste, and modernity.

RELATED ENTRIES

See also
MIUCCIA PRADA
page 64

SEASONS
page 78

SHOWS
page 80

READY-TO-WEAR
page 102

3-SECOND BIOGRAPHIES

GIORGIO ARMANI
1934–
Influential fashion designer whose Armani brand was established in Milan in 1975

GIANNI VERSACE
1946–97
Fashion designer whose Milan-based Versace brand epitomizes contemporary Italian fashion

EXPERT

Julia Rea

Milan forms an urban backdrop to Italian fashion's high-octane brand of glamor and luxury.

1949
Born in Milan, Italy

1978
Takes over her family's luxury leather goods company

1985
Launches her first successful handbag line under the Prada name

1989
Produces the first ready-to-wear womenswear line for Prada

1992
Launches a more affordable secondary line, Miu Miu

1993
Wins International Designer of the Year, awarded by the Council of Fashion Designers of America; founds contemporary art foundation Fondazione Prada

2012
Subject of major exhibition *Schiaparelli and Prada: Impossible Conversations* alongside late designer Elsa Schiaparelli at the Metropolitan Museum of Art, New York

2013
Awarded the inaugural International Designer of the Year at the British Fashion Awards

MIUCCIA PRADA

Miuccia Prada remains one of

Italy's most influential contemporary fashion designers, transforming her family's Milanese heritage leather goods company into a powerful global fashion brand. Adopting an intellectual approach to design, Prada's work combines clean lines and classic colors with innovative fabrics and prints to create an aesthetic that unites luxury and wearability. Often disregarding current design trends, her collections draw upon her interests in art, movies, and wider culture.

Initially reluctant to become involved with the luxury luggage business founded by her grandfather in 1913, Prada obtained a doctorate in political science at the University of Milan before training as a mime artist in a Milanese theater. Her love of aesthetics, however, drew her toward design and she came to the helm of the Prada company in 1978, seeking to modernize and reimagine its business structure and aesthetic. In 1985, she launched her first line of bags, a range of utilitarian black nylon handbags and rucksacks that formed the antithesis of the logo-saturated accessories that dominated the fashion landscape of the era. This now iconic range of bags set a precedent for the Prada design aesthetic.

Her first ready-to-wear womenswear line, launched in 1989, was widely criticized for the seemingly lackluster aesthetic of its predominately black palette and minimalistic shapes. However, the collection's understated elegance stood out among a season of bold and bright collections and the powerful yet feminine aesthetic of its functional tailoring made Prada the aspirational label of choice for a new generation of active, modern women.

In 1992, Prada launched a secondary label, Miu Miu, distinguished by its fresher, more whimsical aesthetic, younger target market, and more affordable price point. The label's wit-infused formula of girlish printed dresses, pastel-colored ruched leather handbags, glittered and embellished shoes, and rococo-style costume jewelry embodies a contradictory blend of nostalgia and modernity, projecting a playful image of femininity.

Her passion for contemporary art, architecture, and movies remains at the forefront of her creative vision, projected across the label's designs, shows, and retail spaces. Regular collaborations with photographers and directors have produced iconic advertising imagery and short movies, while her contribution of key dresses to Baz Lurhmann's 2013 movie *The Great Gatsby* cemented the significance of Prada's thoroughly modern reinterpretation of femininity. The global success of the Prada brand draws its strength from its merging of simplicity and luxury, innovation and classicism, continually blurring the boundaries between the conceptual and the commercial.

Julia Rea

TOKYO

Since Japan opened its borders

to the West in 1853, its culture has greatly influenced artists and thinkers alike, but during the 1980s, Tokyo emerged as one of fashion's great capital cities. At this time, three young, Tokyo-based designers began showing at Paris Fashion Week. They were Issey Miyake, Rei Kawakubo (for her label Comme des Garçons), and Yohji Yamamoto. During the 1980s, much of the industry was producing opulent looks in a kaleidoscope of jewel tones. In contrast, Miyake, Kawakubo, and Yamamoto showed rough, worn-looking garments in monochromatic shades of black, white, and gray. Their clothes were loose fitting, unconventionally cut, and often asymmetrical. They used holes and frayed edges as decoration and would "deconstruct" traditional garments and reconstruct them into new and interesting forms—a technique that would become *de rigueur* for cutting-edge fashion in the decades to follow. At first, the press derided their work as "post-atomic" chic, but these three pioneered a conceptual approach to fashion. They challenged Western notions of fit and finish, and, in so doing, solidified Tokyo's position as a hub of fashion's avant-garde. The next generation of designers has continued this legacy, including Undercover's Jun Takahashi, Junya Watanabe, and Sacai's Chitose Abe.

3-SECOND SKETCH
As a hub of both fashion design talent and cutting-edge street-style, Tokyo has positioned itself as one of fashion's most forward-thinking capitals.

3-MINUTE DETAILING
Tokyo is not only hailed for its avant-garde designers, but also for its distinctive street style. The sometimes extreme looks adopted by Tokyo's different style tribes are often a *mélange* of trends and references—these can vary from Victorian childrenswear to Japanese anime (or manga) characters. Each style tribe has its own vocabulary of looks, but they share an interest in experimentation, customization, and attention to detail in the way they dress.

RELATED ENTRIES
See also
REI KAWAKUBO
page 40

STREET PHOTOGRAPHY
page 142

LOLITAS
page 150

3-SECOND BIOGRAPHIES
ISSEY MIYAKE
1938–
Tokyo-based designer

REI KAWAKUBO
1942–
Tokyo-based designer and founder of Comme des Garçons

YOHJI YAMAMOTO
1943–
Tokyo-based designer

EXPERT
Emma McClendon

Tokyo is renowned worldwide for both its avant-garde high fashion and its distinctive street style.

SÃO PAULO

Boasting the largest GDP in Latin America, as well as substantial communities of Italian, Lebanese, and Japanese immigrants, São Paulo is a diverse state and cosmopolitan city. While domestically viewed as a stylish shopping destination, recent global interest has cast it as the epicenter of fashion in South America. Iguatemi São Paulo, the first mall of Brazil, opened in the 1960s, catering to affluent consumers and carrying primarily foreign and luxury retail brands. A function of both security and consumer desire, the bulk of Brazilian retail fashion is concentrated and consumed in malls. The growth of the middle class has spurred the development of malls that feature local and low-cost apparel brands. Stores such as Lojas Riachuelo, Lojas Renner, and Lojas Marisa stand alongside international players such as Topshop, Gap, and Zara. Brazil's most densely populated metropolis also plays host to São Paulo Fashion Week, the fifth largest behind London, Paris, New York, and Milan respectively. Founded in 1996, this biannual affair draws nearly a million visitors and showcases the work of more than forty Brazil-based designers. Alexandre Herchcovitch, PatBo, and Uma all create garments that have drawn an international audience and counter the dismissive assertion that only swimwear is produced in South America.

3-SECOND SKETCH
In recent decades, São Paulo has established itself on the global fashion map.

3-MINUTE DETAILING
The fashion industry is often charged with presenting too narrow a vision of beauty, and one that fails to represent the diversity of an increasingly global audience. In 2009, São Paulo Fashion Week enacted requirements to ensure that at least 10 percent of models be "black or indigenous" as a way to foster diversity.

RELATED ENTRIES
See also
MODELS
page 82

READY-TO-WEAR
page 102

3-SECOND BIOGRAPHIES
ALEXANDRE HERCHCOVITCH
1971–
Central Saint Martins graduate and influential Brazilian designer who started his eponymous line in 1994

GISELE BÜNDCHEN
1980–
The world's highest-paid model chose the Spring 2015 Colcci show during São Paulo Fashion Week to retire from modeling

EXPERT
Rebecca Straub

From models to fashion designers, Brazilians play a role in shaping the look of fashion both inside and outside of South America.

ORDEM E PROGRESSO

INDIA

In a country with a rich history

of textile production that stretches back to the domestication of cotton in 4000 BCE, contemporary Indian designers push at the boundaries of traditional dress by imagining new possibilities for hand embroidery and other time-honored practices. The Fashion Design Council of India, a not-for-profit organization charged with "promoting, nurturing, and representing the best of fashion design," created Lakme Fashion Week in 1999. The biannual event takes place in Mumbai and honors the council's commitment to promote Indian designers. By dressing some of Bollywood's leading men and women, designers such as Manish Malhotra and Tarun Tahiliani use the popularity and visibility of Hindi cinema—a $1.9 billion industry—to market their designs. Payal Singhal, Nikhil Thampi, and Gaurav Gupta stand out for their use of traditional methods of embellishment. Yet they use lavishly hand-embroidered details on modern, even futuristically shaped garments. Displaying such a high degree of craftsmanship and sumptuous ornamentation serves the dual function of creating garments that meet the demands of the Indian wedding and sari market, while also distinguishing their work in the international marketplace.

RELATED ENTRIES
See also
SHOWS
page 80

3-SECOND SKETCH
Contemporary Indian designers create clothing that responds to a global market for fashion without sacrificing traditional methods of production.

3-MINUTE DETAILING
Worldwide, the Indian wedding market is a $20 billion industry. Demand for *lenghas*, *sherwanis*, and wedding jewelry from both inside and outside the country has spurred investment in e-commerce sites. Exclusively.in, one of the largest online Indian apparel retailers, maintains a dedicated wedding boutique and is active on social media. Customers can purchase Indian-sourced garments and post wedding photos to the Facebook page, which serve as the best advertisement for Exclusively's wares.

3-SECOND BIOGRAPHIES
MANISH MALHOTRA
1965–
Model turned designer responsible for redefining the look of Bollywood costume in Indian cinema

GAURAV GUPTA
1979–
Central Saint Martins graduate hailed internationally as "The Future of Couture," and India's brightest fashion star

NIKHIL THAMPI
1986–
Favorite designer among Bollywood actresses

EXPERT
Rebecca Straub

Indian craftsmanship combines with creative impulses to produce garments that aim to satisfy the needs of a global marketplace.

CHINA

Clothing in China has long been used to express status and political affiliation, as well as personal style. In the seventeenth century, Manchu-Qing rulers asserted their authority over the Han population by creating strict rules for imperial dress, and in the twentieth century the Mao suit came to represent the dissolution of class distinctions promised under communism. Amid the growth of China's middle class and accompanying consumer culture, the Chinese fashion industry has flourished in the twenty-first century. Luxury brands including Louis Vuitton and Michael Kors have opened stores in mainland China, and Chinese tourists represent the fastest-growing demographic for luxury spending. Yet these high-end retailers face strong competition from contemporary Chinese designers. In 1997, China established its own fashion week, creating a public stage to showcase homegrown talent. Brands such as Dancing Wolves, SUN TOMORROW, and Merisis take to Beijing's runways twice a year to show their work. In 2005, Condé Nast started *Vogue China*. "*Vogue China* readers are mostly working women, dressing is only a small part of their lives, so I have to capture the other parts," stated the magazine's Editor-in-Chief, Angelica Cheung, describing an audience eager to absorb high fashion as one of many contemporary pursuits.

3-SECOND SKETCH
China both produces and consumes much of the world's fashion. It embodies the complicated relationship the fashion industry has with the production of its goods.

3-MINUTE DETAILING
As the manufacturer of much of the world's ready-to-wear clothing, the global fashion industry could not operate at the speed and with the reach it currently achieves without Chinese labor. Yet, describing fashion only in terms of sweatshops and the multinational companies that employ them obscures the aesthetic innovation that the Chinese fashion industry now fosters, and ignores the influence traditional Chinese dress and art have always had on the West.

RELATED ENTRIES
See also
READY-TO-WEAR
page 102

3-SECOND BIOGRAPHIES
ANGELICA CHEUNG
1966–
Editor-in-Chief of *Vogue China*

WU XINJIAO
Dates unknown
Design director of Hangzhou Initial Life Fashion, and SUN TOMORROW

LI NA
Dates unknown
Head designer for Merisis

EXPERT
Rebecca Straub

China's rich history of dress and manufacture can be seen in the work of its contemporary fashion designers including Merisis (top), Dancing Wolves (bottom left), and RanFan (bottom right).

THE FASHION CALENDAR

THE FASHION CALENDAR
GLOSSARY

atelier The workshop or studio of a designer and where couture garments are made.

cruise collection Also known as the resort collection, this is an additional fashion collection shown in November between the traditional spring/summer and fall/winter collections. Originally focused on ready-to-wear holiday and leisure clothing for clients spending the winter in sunnier climes, it has become an increasingly important collection financially, for fashion houses.

fashion week A fashion week is not always a week long: Paris spring/summer 2016 was nine days long, for example. But it is the short period when the designers in New York, London, Milan, and Paris show off their new collections twice yearly, consecutively, city by city, to assorted media, buyers, clients, and celebrities, hopefully garnering further press coverage and exposure. Fashion weeks are now held globally, with São Paulo, Sydney, and Beijing, for example, all making their mark.

haute couture Literally "elite sewing," the haute couture house is based in Paris and is a member of the *Chambre Syndicale de la Haute Couture*. Garments are bespoke, fitted directly to the client, and made by seamstresses from the drawings or ideas of the chief designer before being embellished, for example, with embroidery or beadwork.

mannequin The live model used to display clothes, either at a runway show or within an atelier. Can also refer to a dummy used to display clothes, for example, in a store window.

precollection Originally known as the resort or cruise collection, now increasingly commercially important for designers during the winter months, before the spring/summer collections are delivered. The focus is on wearable, accessible clothes with little seasonal emphasis, as it is also for the transitional prefall collection, presented in May. These collections also give a chance for designers to try out ideas and color palettes before presenting their main collections, which garner more publicity. The expansion of these collections shows their economic significance for fashion houses.

ready-to-wear Clothing that is mass-manufactured in standard sizes and bought by a consumer without prefitting or individual preordering—that is the majority of clothing bought by consumers today.

resort collection *See* cruise collection and precollection.

runway A long, narrow, usually elevated platform, or stage, which models walk along to show off a collection during a fashion show. Also shorthand for showing off a new look.

supermodel A highly successful fashion model who has walked the haute couture runways as well as having commercial appeal for advertisers and press. They have global recognition and celebrity, not just in the fashion world, and so, are often known by just their first name.

tastemaker A person, or small group, whose opinions and judgments are accepted and followed by many other people, so that their ideas enter mainstream fashion.

waif Fragile, thin, young, and childlike, the waif look has had various incarnations from Twiggy in the 1960s to Kate Moss in the 1990s.

SEASONS

3-SECOND SKETCH
Dividing designers' collections into defined seasons facilitates a system in which the designers can work together with buyers and press to optimize the market's current demands.

3-MINUTE DETAILING
The increasing pace of the fashion industry has led to the introduction of inter-season collections to bridge the six-month gap between the two main seasonal collections. These typically more commercial precollections are divided into cruise or resort collections, which arose from a demand for lighter summer clothing for winter travel, and transitional prefall collections. Becoming available in November and May respectively, precollections reflect the increasing mutability of fashion's seasonal definitions.

The fashion industry operates on a specific calendar that is divided into defined "seasons," driven by the necessity of forming an efficient marketing and distribution system that unites the separate spheres of designers, retail buyers, and the fashion press. Traditionally, the two annual seasons are defined as spring/summer and fall/winter, with each one producing seasonally appropriate collections in line with the market's current demands. The positioning of each season within the calendar year, however, is complex. Each season centers around a calendar of fashion weeks, held consecutively across the four primary fashion centers—New York, London, Milan, and Paris—during which designers present their latest collections through fashion shows attended by buyers, editors, and high-profile clients. These are typically staged six months prior to the collection becoming available to purchase, resulting in a fashion season cycle that runs in reverse order to the calendar year, with spring/summer collections usually being shown in September and October, and fall/winter collections customarily premiering across February and March. Each season's collections are broken down into more specific categories, with menswear collections usually held one month prior to womenswear, and womenswear divided into haute couture and ready-to-wear.

EXPERT
Julia Rea

Fashion seasons run in reverse order to most calendar seasons. This system promotes the prompt turnover of product and ensures the efficient coordination of a commercial structure that incorporates every facet of the industry.

SHOWS

The most significant event in the fashion industry calendar, the runway show is the medium through which designers present their latest collections to press, buyers, high-profile clients, and influential fashion editors. The show's primary purpose is promotion, as designers present their work in the most desirable mode possible to generate sales, secure positive reviews, and build the profile and identity of their brand. The concept of the fashion show has its roots in the couture houses of early twentieth-century Paris, where in-house models presented the latest designs for a limited audience of clients and buyers. However, over the course of the century, the show's format evolved into increasingly large-scale theatrical performances involving elaborate sets, lighting effects, meticulous model casting, and spectacle. Contemporary fashion shows aim to generate excitement and anticipation around a collection and designer, seducing its influential audience with narrative, novelty, and innovation. Rather than detracting focus from the garments, the design of a show endeavors to complement a collection's aesthetic and bring its philosophy to life, creating memorable imagery and developing a coherent creative vision. Emerging designers on more limited budgets opt for simpler, minimalistic "presentations" to promote their designs, often relying on sponsorship contracts.

3-SECOND SKETCH

Runway shows present a collection through a lens of emotion and seduction in order to memorably evoke its essence and themes and gain maximum publicity.

3-MINUTE DETAILING

Through the medium of storytelling, shows construct fantasies of escapism and desire that belie fashion's commercial reality. Alexander McQueen became well known for dramatic spectacles that referenced his diverse inspirations, from wintery snowscapes and cascading fire to subaquatic worlds and life-size chessboards. Similarly, Karl Lagerfeld has pushed the creative and practical boundaries of the show, setting his garments against the backdrops of makeshift interactive grocery stores and sending his models on a faux feminist protest.

RELATED ENTRIES
See also
SEASONS
page 78

MODELS
page 82

HAIR & MAKEUP
page 90

FRONT ROW
page 92

STYLISTS
page 128

3-SECOND BIOGRAPHIES
PAUL POIRET
1879–1944
Designer who was the first to stage a presentation exclusively for the press in 1910

KARL LAGERFELD
1933–
Creative Director of Chanel and Fendi who revolutionized the runway show with innovative settings

EXPERT
Julia Rea

Alexander McQueen was renowned for the theatricality of his runway shows.

MODELS

RELATED ENTRIES
See also
SHOWS
page 80

In the eighteenth and nineteenth centuries dressmakers' dolls and scaled-down mannequins were used to showcase the latest fashions. However, as early as the 1840s, Parisian dressmakers began employing living mannequins to parade before clients in order to show how clothes appeared in movement. Throughout the twentieth century, models became the preeminent subjects of fashion photography and shows. These increasingly public figures demonstrated how to style, move, and pose in the latest fashions. In the early 1990s, the original supermodels—Linda Evangelista, Naomi Campbell, Christy Turlington, and Claudia Schiffer—achieved worldwide celebrity status, as they starred in both lucrative commercial campaigns and high-fashion editorial features. When the teenage, waiflike British model Kate Moss rose to fame in the mid-1990s, she was presented by the media as the grungy antithesis to the glamorous supermodels. Moss, who soon developed an eclectic personal style, later became known for her self-authored transformations. The rise of social media in the twenty-first century has enabled younger models, notably Cara Delevingne, Karlie Kloss, and Jourdan Dunn, to follow Moss's example and employ an unprecedented degree of autonomy over their public image.

3-SECOND BIOGRAPHIES

CHRISTY TURLINGTON
1969–
American model

NAOMI CAMPBELL
1970–
British model

KATE MOSS
1974–
British model

JOAN SMALLS
1988–
Puerto Rican model

CARA DELEVINGNE
1992–
British model

EXPERT

Katerina Pantelides

Contemporary models are celebrated for their individual looks, but are at the same time required to be versatile enough to embody the designer's vision.

BUYERS

Fashion buyers select the pieces from ready-to-wear collections that will be sold in stores. They are one of fashion's "gate keepers," who decide what will actually become available to consumers. Within the fashion calendar, buyers purchase stock from designers during four seasonal market weeks: spring, prefall, fall, and resort. These market weeks occur immediately following official fashion weeks in fall and spring—the idea is to have buyers purchase pieces within days of a collection's runway show. Once all buyers have selected stock from a collection, the collection is put into production with garments reaching retail locations up to six months later. Buyers purchase pieces "wholesale" directly from designers at a price called "cost." A buyer must negotiate the mark-up that a garment will get in-store to make a "retail" price. This mark-up is the life-blood of all stores. Buyers can work for any type of retailer from large-scale department stores, to small boutiques and e-commerce sites. Designer companies will even have in-house buyers to select stock for their flagship stores. Buyers are generally responsible for a particular category of clothing, such as womenswear, menswear, or childrenswear, but can be more specialized in large retailers. They are responsible for knowing the taste of their client base as well as keeping up with current trends.

RELATED ENTRIES
See also
SEASONS
page 78

SHOWS
page 80

READY-TO-WEAR
page 102

3-SECOND SKETCH
Buyers take fashion from the runway to the retail floor and control what consumers can own.

3-MINUTE DETAILING
While buyers are typically behind-the-scenes forces in the fashion industry, some rise to become defining figures for a store or company's public brand. Such figures include Lord & Taylor's Dorothy Shaver, who put the American department store on the national stage when she decided to market home-grown, American designers in the 1930s and 1940s. Another famous buyer-in-charge is Bergdorf Goodman's Linda Fargo, who is known as the famed retailer's "eyes" for her forward-thinking taste.

3-SECOND BIOGRAPHIES
DOROTHY SHAVER
1893–1959
Retail executive for Lord & Taylor in New York

LINDA FARGO
1961–
Senior Vice President of Bergdorf Goodman in New York

EXPERT
Emma McClendon

Buyers are part of the intricate behind-the-scenes world of fashion and determine everything, from which clothes make it to stores to when styles will go on sale.

1949
Born in London, England

1964
First fashion industry job at Biba boutique in London

1970
First job in fashion journalism at *Harpers & Queen* in London

1976
Moves to New York to work for *Harper's Bazaar*, *New York* magazine, and eventually *Vogue*

1985
Returns to London to take job as Editor-in-Chief at British *Vogue*

1987
Moves back to New York to work for *House & Garden* magazine

1988
Named Editor-in-Chief at American *Vogue*

2008
Appointed an officer of the Order of the British Empire (OBE)

2013
Named Artistic Director for the entirety of Condé Nast

2014
Metropolitan Museum of Art's Costume Institute renamed the Anna Wintour Costume Center

ANNA WINTOUR

Anna Wintour is often described as the most powerful woman in fashion. She is best known for her position as Editor-in-Chief of American *Vogue*, which she has held since 1988. But as fashion journalist Dana Thomas describes, Wintour is more than an editor: she "was and is fashion's kingmaker ... she [can] make or break a career by choosing who appears in the editorial pages of her magazine, she advises designers on what to design and where to work and counsels company executives on who to hire." Wintour is now not only Editor-in-Chief of American *Vogue*, but also Artistic Director for the entirety of Condé Nast. She also sits on the board of the Metropolitan Museum of Art where she donated enough funds to the Costume Institute to have it renamed the Anna Wintour Costume Center in 2014.

Born to the former Editor-in-Chief of London's *Evening Standard*, Charles Wintour, Anna took an interest in fashion from a young age. With the help of her father, she secured a job at the trendy boutique Biba at the height of London's 1960s "youth quake." She was just 15 years old. Anna worked only on Saturdays so as not to interfere with her schoolwork, but that short time was enough to have a profound effect on her career. When she was 16, Anna dropped out of North London Collegiate School to enroll in a training programme at the historic London retailer Harrods. According to fashion legend, the catalyst for Anna's departure from school was when, to the horror of her teachers, she showed up to class wearing a daring mini-skirt, cut well above the knee.

Wintour's first foray into fashion journalism was at the London publication *Harpers & Queen* in 1970. A few years later, she moved to New York where she worked for *Harper's Bazaar*, *New York* magazine, and eventually American *Vogue* before returning to London in 1985 to head British *Vogue*. Once there, Wintour made sweeping staff changes and shifted the content of the magazine toward a new demographic, which earned her the nickname "Nuclear Wintour." In 1987, Wintour moved back to New York to run the Condé Nast publication *House & Garden*. It was from here that she was plucked to run American *Vogue* in 1988. Once installed as Editor, Wintour wasted no time making similar staff and content changes as those she had made at British *Vogue*. Her first cover has become a symbol of this shift. In it, Wintour decided to feature a virtually unknown model wearing a luxuriously embellished Christian Lacroix jacket paired with—shockingly—stonewashed jeans. This mix of high-end and low-end pieces is just one example of Anna Wintour's forward-thinking vision that has made her a leader in the industry.

Emma McClendon

EDITORS

RELATED ENTRIES
See also
THE GLOSSIES
page 120

EDITORIAL
page 122

Editors are the "gate keepers" of
the fashion media. They can work for a variety
of publications including glossy magazines,
television, websites, and newspapers. The
specific role of an editor varies greatly
depending on the type of media outlet he or
she works for. However, an editor's duties often
include developing content for articles, features,
and photo shoots, as well as researching future
topics and trends. Editors report on fashion
news and events throughout the year. Within
the fashion calendar, editors attend the
seasonal runway shows in force—indeed, getting
an editor's attention can be a make-or-break
moment for a designer. Editors for "short lead"
media outlets such as newspapers, websites,
and television stations publish runway reports
concurrently with, or immediately after official
fashion weeks. Editors for "long lead" press,
on the other hand, work up to six months in
advance of a publication date. Rather than
writing reviews, editors for long lead
publications such as the glossy magazines
Vogue and *Harper's Bazaar* often translate
runway looks into multi-page photography
spreads. These spreads can focus on a trendy
stylistic element, such as "stripes" or "flared
pants," or draw on more fantasy driven themes
such as "fairy tales" or "futurism."

3-SECOND BIOGRAPHIES
CARMEL SNOW
1887–1961
Editor-in-Chief of *Harper's Bazaar* 1934–58

DIANA VREELAND
1903–89
Editor-in-Chief of American *Vogue* 1963–71

ANDRÉ LEON TALLEY
1949–
Editor-at-Large at American *Vogue* for nearly three decades

HAMISH BOWLES
1963–
Editor at American *Vogue* since 1995

EXPERT
Emma McClendon

Great editors, such as Hamish Bowles, rely on their impeccable eye and are often trendsetters themselves.

HAIR & MAKEUP

The role of the makeup artist

and hair stylist extends beyond merely adding decorative finishing touches to a designer's collection, with their skills and own creative vision being instrumental in constructing a coherent image of a collection's themes. Working closely alongside the designer, show producer, and stylists, the hair and makeup teams are responsible for visually interpreting these themes through the employment of different makeup techniques and color palettes, hairstyles, wigs, and headpieces. This complex backstage process requires an efficient system of seamless coordination, planning, and communication, working quickly in order to prepare the models in the shortest amount of time possible, usually taking several hours. Preshow preparation involves closely studying the whole collection and liaising directly with the designer and can vary from several weeks to a few days in advance depending on the complexity of the desired result. A series of meticulous trials then follow before the designer approves a finished "look" and the team feels confident that it can be realistically achieved with the time and resources available.

RELATED ENTRIES

See also
SHOWS
page 80

MODELS
page 82

STYLISTS
page 128

3-SECOND BIOGRAPHIES

KENNETH BATTELLE
1927–2013
Hair stylist credited as the first celebrity hairdresser

GUIDO PALAU
1962–
Hair stylist with long-term relationships with leading designers

PAT MCGRATH
1966–
Makeup artist described by *Vogue* as the most influential in the industry

EXPERT
Julia Rea

3-SECOND SKETCH
A fashion show's hair and makeup teams bring a designer's creative vision to life, projecting and connecting both the collection's specific themes and the brand's wider identity.

3-MINUTE DETAILING
Global makeup and haircare brands frequently use established makeup artists and hair stylists as creative directors and consultants, where they oversee the development of products, style advertising imagery, and promote their brands through their usage on runway shows and editorial photo shoots. Prominent industry figures, such as Pat McGrath at Gucci and Guido Palau at Redken, bring both their expertise and influence to these collaborations, forming mutually beneficial partnerships.

Hair and makeup define the projected identity of models and create the desired aesthetic.

FRONT ROW

The front row of a fashion show

is where the most important guests sit. These include prominent members of the fashion press, major buyers, and celebrities who the brand wishes to be associated with. Front-row guests do not only have an optimal view of the collections, but also receive significant media attention. Brands have sought to strike a balance between having enough celebrities in the front row to create an atmosphere of exclusivity and incite media interest, and making sure that the collections themselves receive sufficient coverage. Thus, brands have oscillated between the extremes of paying celebrities up to $80,000 for attendance, and staging secret shows, with 100 guests and a front row undocumented by the media, as Tom Ford did for his spring/summer 2011 collection. Alexander McQueen famously antagonized the front row in his spring/summer 2001 collection "Voss," where he positioned the overweight, naked Michelle Olley in a glass case of moths to bring guests face to face with fashion's enemies: fat and fabric predators. Then the case turned into mirrored glass, so that the fashion-conscious guests would have to scrutinize themselves. However, fashion-show seating arrangements continue to be a media obsession, because their hierarchical nature generates an impression of guests' fashionability and commercial importance.

RELATED ENTRIES
See also
ALEXANDER MCQUEEN
page 26

SHOWS
page 80

ANNA WINTOUR
page 86

3-SECOND BIOGRAPHIES
ANNA WINTOUR
1949–
Editor of American *Vogue*

TOM FORD
1961–
Designer

ALEXANDER MCQUEEN
1969–2010
Designer who arranged elaborate, often controversial shows

EXPERT
Katerina Pantelides

Anna Wintour is a desired front-row guest, because she is considered a prime tastemaker both within and beyond fashion circles.

FROM COUTURE TO MAIN STREET

FROM COUTURE TO MAIN STREET
GLOSSARY

atelier The workshop or studio of a designer and where couture garments are made.

bespoke A garment made to order, specifically for a certain customer, and using that customer's precise measurements for fitting the garment. The process will usually involve several fittings to ensure a perfect fit and finish.

capsule collection When a limited supply of garments, usually a collaboration between a fashion store and designer or celebrity, is released as a collection. It can also be a few key items of clothing by the same designer that can be used in various permutations to achieve different looks and be added to with more seasonal pieces.

fast fashion Around since the 1960s, but getting increasingly faster with advances in technology, this is the ability of retailers to respond quickly to new trends and styles on the runway, and today also on social media, and reproduce these in clothing for their customers in as short a time as possible. Such clothing is low-cost and is likely to be disposed of once the trend has run its course.

hip-hop From roots in mid-1970s New York, hip-hop began to reach the mainstream during the 1980s, with its music, a combination of DJs and MCs, and an uncompromising urban street style. Aspirational dressing, in the form of elite sportswear brands and high-end designers, has become a key part of the look.

petites mains Translated as "little hands," these are the skilled artisans who work on the couture garment under the guidance of the designer.

Mod A shortening of "Modernist," Mods emerged in the late 1950s and early 1960s and sought to demonstrate good taste and the "less is more" ethos of sharp, "cool" dressing based on Italian style. Subsequent revivals of the style have led to a caricature "Mod" style emerging.

slow fashion A movement working toward sustainable fashion and raising awareness of the ecological and social impact of the production of clothing within a global context. With its opposition to mass-produced, "fast," and cheap clothing it seeks to find alternatives not so reliant on seasonal trends, including clothing already in circulation, for example, secondhand or upcycled pieces.

sweatshop A factory or workshop where manual workers are employed for long hours with low pay and under poor conditions, sometimes dangerously, with very few workers' rights. Local laws may also have been violated, for instance, the use of child labor or disregarding minimum wage pay levels, with workers exploited to produce cheap goods for manufacturers, usually to sell to the West.

Teddy Boy A youth movement that emerged post-Second World War, for the newly defined teenager, Teddy Boys first appeared in working-class south London. The look required head-to-toe dressing and drew inspiration from tailoring harking back to the Edwardian era, a style then being produced on Savile Row. Longer length jackets, flamboyant vests, and velvet trim were popular, partly as a reaction to postwar austerity, mixed with American influences such as the cowboy's "maverick" tie.

three-piece suit A coat or jacket, vest, and pants or skirt made from the same material throughout and worn together as one outfit, a style which has evolved from its origins in the 1660s.

upcycling The creative reuse of discarded or unwanted clothing and/or textiles, making something new, and perhaps better than the original.

vintage Generally perceived to be clothing more than twenty years old. As such, clothing will often be secondhand but representative and immediately recognizable as fashion that originated from a particular decade of the twentieth century.

HAUTE COUTURE

According to French law, clothes

are only deemed to be haute couture if they are approved by the Chambre Syndicale de la Haute Couture. This legislative organization ensures that couture houses possess a Paris-based workshop, which employs at least fifteen full-time members of staff, present daywear and formal-wear collections biannually before the press, and create bespoke garments that are directly fitted to clients' bodies. The clothes are made with a high degree of hand finish by *petites mains*, talented seamstresses who are affiliated to a couture house. Afterward, the embellishmentof garments is typically outsourced to specialist Parisian ateliers, for example, the embroidery workshop Lesage. The first couture house, belonging to Charles Frederick Worth, opened in 1858, and today there are about fifteen couture houses in Paris, including Chanel, Christian Dior, and Givenchy. Haute couture collections are shown to smaller, more exclusive audiences than ready-to-wear, and continue to emphasize craftsmanship and spectacle. However, in the past three decades, couturiers have presented subversive visions of luxury, in collections with overt political and sociological references. Indeed, fashion most approximates art in couture collections, because bespoke production enables the fullest expression of a designer's creativity.

RELATED ENTRIES
See also
PARIS
page 58

SHOWS
page 80

READY-TO-WEAR
page 102

3-SECOND SKETCH
Haute couture translates as "elite sewing," and is the most exclusive branch of fashion, because its custom-made garments sometimes require more than 700 hours of labor.

3-MINUTE DETAILING
Factors including the drastic price increase of haute couture after the Second World War and the popularity of ready-to-wear fashion in the subsequent decades, threatened to drive the couture industry into obscurity. However, detailed media coverage of couture presentations and the prominence of custom-made, intricately embellished garments worn by celebrities at events such as the Academy Awards, have played important roles in reengaging public interest in haute couture.

3-SECOND BIOGRAPHY
CHARLES FREDERICK WORTH
1825–95
Couturier who established the first couture house in 1858 in Paris

EXPERT
Katerina Pantelides

Christian Dior regarded haute couture as a collaboration between the couturier's ideas, the petites mains' industry and the model's talents.

SAVILE ROW

A street in London's Mayfair

area, Savile Row has become synonymous with names such as Gieves & Hawkes, Henry Poole & Co., Hardy Amies, and Anderson & Sheppard. They sum up a particular type of men's tailoring based around the bespoke or made-to-measure suit, a technique that has changed little since the nineteenth century. The suit is made for an individual on an exclusive basis, often with input from the customer. The customer is measured by hand, the pattern is cut by hand, and then the garment is made up in and around the Row, with the process taking around fifty-two hours. The look epitomizes the English gentleman, whether in tweed or pinstripe, and has been worn by royalty, politicians, and movie stars. Henry Poole, who took over a military tailoring business from his father in 1846, was the first to operate from Savile Row, developing the trade to include sporting and civilian clothing. The reinvention of the tradition by Nutters of Savile Row from 1969, and the "New Establishment" tailors Richard James and Ozwald Boateng in the 1990s, has led to a renewed interest in the bespoke suit and English style. The Savile Row Bespoke Association was established in 2004 to promote and protect their trade and name, and their traditions of quality and craftsmanship.

RELATED ENTRIES
See also
MENSWEAR
page 104

3-SECOND SKETCH
The Savile Row style means elegant, bespoke classical men's tailoring, although also sometimes quietly surprising with flamboyant linings or hidden messages, worn by the great and the good.

3-MINUTE DETAILING
Henry Poole was a Victorian master of advertising and product placement, using the celebrities of his day, including the Prince of Wales and sportsmen such as the jockey Jem Mason, to wear his clothes. To be "Pooled" from head to foot was used as a description of his clients. His store was also elaborately decorated for special occasions, drawing in crowds and setting the template for retail promotion.

3-SECOND BIOGRAPHIES
HENRY POOLE
1814–76
Founder of Savile Row and "tailor to all the crowned heads in the world of any note"

HARDY AMIES
1909–2003
Produced tailored clothes for both men and women, including Queen Elizabeth II

OZWALD BOATENG
1967–
The first tailor to stage a runway show in Paris, in 1994

EXPERT
Alison Toplis

From male peacocks to conservative suit wearers, all have been outfitted by Savile Row tailors.

SAVILE ROW W1

CITY OF WESTMINSTER

READY-TO-WEAR

RELATED ENTRIES
See also
MAIN STREET
page 110

EXPERT
Alison Toplis

Ready-to-wear clothing

encompasses the vast majority of clothing bought and worn today: that is, clothing bought from store stock in a standardized size without prefitting. The clothing can be mass produced in factories or manufactured on a smaller scale, but if it is not made with a particular customer in mind, rather to enter the surplus stock of a retailer, it is ready-to-wear. Over the course of the twentieth century, consumers have increasingly been buying clothing not for durability or function but for fashion, so-called "fast" fashion. Ideas from the couture runways are reinterpreted by ready-to-wear designers and manufactured quickly to reach mass markets. Technological developments have increased the speed of the design process so it is no longer only reliant on the biannual couture shows for inspiration, but takes trends from the street and, today, social media. Information gleaned directly from store sales also influences the design process and how retailers order and reorder clothing. Clothing retailers now get new garments to consumers every few weeks and garments can be of a limited run to sell out and encourage buying. "Designer" ready-to-wear offers a broader customer base for couture houses, giving the essence of the designer, although at a more basic level and with a more affordable price tag.

A garment bought ready to put on and wear is the mainstay of the fashion business, from couture houses to budget brands.

MENSWEAR

RELATED ENTRIES
See also
SPORT
page 44

SAVILE ROW
page 100

TEDDY BOYS & GIRLS
page 138

HIP-HOP
page 146

3-SECOND SKETCH

The great masculine renunciation of fashion, the sober dark suit, has never quite taken complete hold and the flamboyant peacock frequently rears his head.

3-MINUTE DETAILING

The first runway show of menswear was shown by Savile Row inhabitant Sir Hardy Amies in 1961. Called "Man," the ready-to-wear collection was shown at the Savoy Hotel, London, with around a dozen models walking to prerecorded music, the designer coming out at the end to take a bow—the first time music and applause had been used and taken in this way. Amies thus set the template for future runway shows.

Tailoring, based around the three-piece suit, has been the foundation of menswear for the last 300 years. However, since the 1960s, designers specializing in men's fashion, rather than traditional tailoring, have emerged. Italian designers, for instance, Nino Cerruti in the 1960s and Giorgio Armani in the 1970s and 1980s, have been particularly influential in menswear, playing on the seductive elegance of the Italian look in contrast to English tradition. Although menswear has been seen as less exciting and more staid than women's fashion, it has absorbed many diverse influences over the last fifty years, from subcultural and street styles including Teddy Boys, Mods, and hip-hop, to sportswear. Designers such as Vivienne Westwood and Alexander McQueen have pushed gender stereotypes by placing men in skirts, and the profile of men's fashion has also shifted, with Hedi Slimane at Dior Homme one of the originators of the influential skinny silhouette for the suit in the first decade of the twenty-first century—a youthful and androgynous look. The reinvigoration of traditional masculine brands such as Louis Vuitton, Dunhill, and Burberry, with designers such as Christopher Bailey at the last, has given a new focus to menswear, which now vies with womenswear in significance at the runway shows.

3-SECOND BIOGRAPHIES
NINO CERRUTI
1930–
Designer who opened his first boutique in Paris in 1967

GIORGIO ARMANI
1934–
A protégé of Cerruti, forming his own company in 1975

EXPERT
Alison Toplis

Although men in skirts have not yet become a mainstream look, menswear designers continue to push the boundaries of the masculine silhouette in other ways.

1946
Born in Nottingham,
England, and educated at
Beeston Fields Grammar
School; leaves school at
15 to work in a clothing
warehouse

1970
Opens first store,
"Paul Smith Vêtements
Pour l'Homme" at
6 Byard Lane,
Nottingham

1979
Opens first London store
in Floral Street, Covent
Garden

1991
Flagship store opens in
Tokyo, making sixty
stores in Japan

1993
Creates womenswear
collection

1994
Awarded a CBE for
services to fashion design

1995
"True Brit" exhibition held
at the Design Museum,
London, celebrating
twenty-five years in
business

2000
Awarded a knighthood
and marries his partner,
Pauline, on the same day

2011
Awarded the
"Outstanding
Achievement in Fashion"
British Fashion Award

2013
"Hello, My Name is
Paul Smith" exhibition
held at the Design
Museum, London

PAUL SMITH

The name "Paul Smith" has come to represent an enormously successful global fashion brand, which is still seen as quintessentially British, a process set in motion over forty years ago in Nottingham by its eponymous founder. Smith's first boutique was opened in the city in 1970, selling rare workwear alongside an eclectic mix of other items, such as stationery found on his travels. Having honed his tailoring skills at night-school and at Savile Row tailors Lincroft Kilgour, Smith began to design clothing to sell in his store, helped by his then girlfriend, later wife, Pauline Denyer, a graduate of the Royal College of Fashion.

By 1976, the Paul Smith look, "classics with a twist," came to fruition, when he showed his first menswear collection in Paris. Based around the relaxed suit, twists included bright linings, his now classic stripy socks, and unusually colored shirts and ties, often with eccentric, humorous prints. His menswear brand expanded dramatically during the 1980s, at home and internationally, particularly in Japan. Realizing that women were buying men's suits to wear, from 1993 he began to develop a women's collection and the brand has continued to expand with childrenswear and collaborations with other companies such as Triumph motorbikes, Anglepoise, and Mini.

He has consistently maintained an individual and independent line, moving outside the vagaries of fashion. His aim has been to produce well-designed clothes that men and women in the street want to wear. He has hinted that awards and headlines in the fashion press, although welcome, are nothing if the business is not commercially viable and that he sees fashion as an industry.

Smith also has a passion for collecting items, often vintage or kitsch, which he will sell on again, alongside clothing, in his stores. These quirky items, for example, old toys, books, vintage crockery, and paper ephemera, have from the beginning given each of his stores a highly individual look and differentiated him from other more corporate designer stores. Customers can buy any of these one-off items that they see alongside the clothes. This sense of being different and of being interesting to the customer, both in terms of the clothes and the store environment, has driven the success of Paul Smith. Playing upon the individuality, quirkiness, and humor of British style, alongside classic English tailoring, Smith's label is commercially successful and critically acclaimed.

Alison Toplis

FRAGRANCES, BEAUTY LINES & ACCESSORIES

The fragrances, beauty lines, and accessories ranges launched by designer brands function as both a lucrative secondary source of income and an effective method of constructing a coherent brand image and identity. Perfumes, makeup, handbags, scarves, jewelry, and other items associated with a design house possess a unique appeal as luxury status objects marketed at a more affordable price point, merging aspiration and accessibility while, simultaneously, heightening the commercial and cultural visibility of a brand. The seductive exclusivity implied by these products signifies an authoritative notion of taste and quality while the significantly weighted value of a designer's name lends the consumer cultural and stylistic "capital": perfume bottles become *objets d'art* and handbags are transformed into ubiquitous icons of design. Luxury brands such as Ralph Lauren and Missoni have expanded their design empires to incorporate homewares and accessories such as candles, translating their distinctive design signatures into a comprehensive lifestyle philosophy. By licensing these products, designers are able to both reach a broader consumer market and financially sustain global businesses that may otherwise be reliant on the more limited scope of the affluent haute couture or ready-to-wear customer.

EXPERT
Julia Rea

Designer accessories occasionally attain iconic status, being positioned as cultural artifacts with an enduring investment appeal.

MAIN STREET

RELATED ENTRIES
See also
READY-TO-WEAR
page 102

COLLABORATIONS
page 112

ETHICAL ISSUES
page 114

3-SECOND BIOGRAPHIES
DONALD FISHER & DORIS
FISHER
1928–2009 & 1932–
Cofounders of US chain
The Gap

LUCIANO BENETTON
1935–
Founder of Italian chain
Benetton

PHILIP GREEN
1952–
Chairman of the Arcadia Group,
which includes Topshop

3-SECOND SKETCH
Branching out firstly into
mail order, now online
shopping, the chain store
caters for everyone and
every pocket.

3-MINUTE DETAILING
With its origin in arcades
and covered bazaars, the
first enclosed shopping
mall was opened in 1956,
near Minneapolis. A natural
home for fashion chain
stores, the mall proliferated
across the West in the late
twentieth century,
particularly in suburban
areas. The mall is now
seen across all continents,
bringing Western clothing
brands to all corners of the
world and homogeny to
fashion consumption.
Whether this should be
entirely welcomed is
another question.

Chain stores, stores with multiple
branches, have developed over the course of
the nineteenth and twentieth centuries, some
from market stalls, and others from department
stores. In competition with boutiques,
independent stores, and department stores,
the chain store will stock a selection of ready-to-
wear fashion, usually aimed at a particular type
or range of consumers, at relatively cheap prices.
Stores dealing specifically in fashion were a
postwar development, catering to the spending
power of the new "teenager," particularly during
the 1960s. In the late twentieth century, the
Italian retailer Benetton and the American
retailer The Gap found huge international
success, the latter offering a version of the
American preppy look. After a hiatus, the market
has been reinvigorated by new names such as
Mango and Zara from Spain and collaborations
with designers and models. The sector is
increasingly diverse in both style and price point
with chains such as J. Crew and Reiss offering
high-end clothing and a particular look, in
contrast to budget chains such as Primark and
Target, which provide cheap basics and their own
take on fashion. Today, styles influenced by the
runway, and sometimes designed by fashion
house stars, are within financial and geographical
reach of the majority of consumers.

EXPERT
Alison Toplis

*For those on a budget,
main street is the place
where fashion dreams
are transformed into
garment reality.*

COLLABORATIONS

Collaborations between high

fashion designers and main street retailers have become hugely successful in the last decade, launching the term "high-low" (or "high end—low end"). American mega-retailer Target first launched its limited-edition collaborations in 2003 with a capsule collection by Isaac Mizrahi. In the ensuing years, Target's series of collaborations with such fashion powerhouses as Missoni, Peter Pilotto, and Joseph Altuzarra regularly sell out hours after being released. Likewise, Swedish fast-fashion company H&M, which began its designer collaborations in 2004 with Karl Lagerfeld, has had phenomenal success with them. Its list of collaborators includes such notable figures as Alexander Wang, Alber Elbaz of Lanvin, and Versace. In some cases, the H&M collaboration launch days have been so successful that customers have had to wait hours just to get into the stores. These high-low collaborations have brought high fashion to a new consumer base. Previously, these brands would have been inaccessible, if not wholly unknown, to the average person. Of course, the garments produced for these collaborations are quite different from their luxury counterparts. Design elements are modified to meet the production requirements of fast-fashion factories and the price tag requirement of fast-fashion consumers.

RELATED ENTRIES
See also
HAUTE COUTURE
page 98

READY-TO-WEAR
page 102

MAIN STREET
page 110

3-SECOND BIOGRAPHIES
ROY HALSTON FROWICK
1932–90
Fashion designer known for his minimalist designs

KARL LAGERFELD
1933–
Creative Director for Chanel, Fendi and his eponymous label

ISAAC MIZRAHI
1961–
Fashion designer and television personality

EXPERT
Emma McClendon

Collaborations have changed the hierarchy of the fashion industry. Today, anyone can own a piece of "designer" clothing.

3-SECOND SKETCH
Collaborations between high fashion designers and main street retailers have democratized the luxury industry and opened the fashion world up to the everyday consumer.

3-MINUTE DETAILING
Collaborations have not always been successful. In 1984, American designer Halston collaborated with mainstream retailer J.C. Penney to produce a line called Halston III. When it debuted, some of Halston's most important high-end retailers, including Bergdorf Goodman, dropped Halston's main line. They felt he had tarnished the exclusivity of his brand. Sadly, J.C. Penney consumers were not interested in purchasing cheap Halstons either. Soon after the failure, Halston was ousted from his own company.

ETHICAL ISSUES

Ethical issues in fashion today

are broad and diverse, from how textiles are produced, including the environmental impact on the surrounding landscape and the effects of globalization, to how the factories that weave the cloth and make the clothes operate. The move of manufacturing from the West to Asia has brought consumers cheap "fast" fashion, but at the expense of low wages and poor working conditions for the factory workers, including the use of child labor. The collapse of the Rana Plaza factory building near Dhaka in Bangladesh in 2013, which killed more than a thousand people, shocked Western commentators with the conditions that the employees worked in making garments for Western retailers. While there is now more awareness, particularly of building safety, there seem to have been few changes in Asian workers' conditions or the mainstream attitudes of Western consumers. However, the "slow fashion" movement has been gaining momentum, promoting sustainable clothing over mass-consumption, for example, wearing secondhand or vintage clothing. In the United States alone, anywhere between eleven and fifteen million tons of clothing is thrown away every year, which suggests recycling or upcycling are increasingly important choices.

3-SECOND SKETCH
As they have come under increasing scrutiny from consumers and the media, fashion companies have adopted ethical policies to create a responsible foundation on which to build their collections.

3-MINUTE DETAILING
Animal welfare also falls under the umbrella of ethical issues, with designers such as Stella McCartney refusing to work with fur and leather in her company. Sustainability is also part of her ethos, and she has continued to win numerous fashion awards while still heading an "honest" and "responsible" company. She has supported PETA, the animal welfare organization, whose campaigns include the famous "I'd Rather Go Naked than Wear Fur" series.

RELATED ENTRIES
See also
MAIN STREET
page 110

3-SECOND BIOGRAPHY
STELLA MCCARTNEY
1971–
Designer, famous for her ethical stance

EXPERT
Alison Toplis

The hidden costs of a garment, whether environmental or ethical, are an increasingly important issue for consumers.

THE MEDIA

blog A webpage that is regularly updated by an individual, or small group of people, usually focused on a particular subject, their opinions, or interests, and which welcomes comments and interaction with readers. Fashion blogs naturally focus on various facets of the fashion industry and use lots of images. The immediate feedback they provide, for example on designer collections, has become particularly influential.

color-blocking Wearing two or more, usually bold and bright, contrasting colors in one outfit. These can be separate pieces put together or a garment designed with blocks of solid color, without any print or pattern.

editorial These are photographs that are commissioned by, and published in, magazines and newspapers. They support the written word alongside them and will often tell a story or communicate an idea through a series of photographs. They sit alongside advertising photography, particularly in magazines.

front row Closest to the runway at a fashion show, the front row is the most prestigious place to be seated and, by default, a way of telling who is most influential in the fashion world for that particular designer. Generally the front row is reserved for the most important fashion editors and a designer's celebrity clients, who may garner media coverage for the collection.

glossy magazine Printed on high-quality, shiny paper, these magazines focus on elite fashion, including couture and ready-to-wear, supported by pages of high-end advertising. They present color images of the current collections, often shot by renowned photographers and worn by famous models and help shape the season for mainstream fashion. *Vogue* and *Harper's Bazaar* are perhaps the best-known titles and have longevity, with both magazines having been published for more than a hundred years.

New Look Christian Dior's first solo collection shown in Paris in February 1947, which featured very full skirts falling from a cinched waist and sloping shoulders, was referred to as the "New Look" by fashion editors present for the show. The feminine look and copious use of fabric contrasted starkly with the wartime austerity and clothes rationing that contemporaries were used to.

September issue For a fashion magazine, traditionally the most important, and biggest, issue of the year. It launches the new fall/winter collections and, in a way, a new fashion year.

signature style The unique way that an individual dresses which then becomes immediately identifiable as belonging only to that person. It expresses their aesthetics and their public persona and may in turn, influence others if, for example, they are well-known or work in the fashion industry.

social media An umbrella term for internet media that allows users to interact, share, and exchange information, whether text, video, images, or other multimedia, and create social and professional online networks.

stylist A stylist is a curator, responsible for coordinating the whole outfit, from clothing to accessories, selecting pieces that will work well both together and on the body of the person wearing it. They can work in many different areas from runway shows to magazine editorial shoots and collaborate with designers, photographers, makeup artists, and art directors, to ensure the best visual image possible.

Web 2.0 A term given to the gradual development of the World Wide Web, which now allows interaction and collaboration, with the building of web-based communities such as blogging and social media, rather than just the passive viewing of content.

THE GLOSSIES

RELATED ENTRIES
See also
EDITORS
page 88

ADVERTISING
page 124

STYLE MAGAZINES
page 126

3-SECOND SKETCH
As a group of luxury
fashion publications,
"the glossies" present an
authoritative curation of
current fashion trends,
in order to create desire,
pleasure, and meaning.

Deriving their collective term
from the glossed paper on which they are
printed, "the glossies" are a select group of
high-end luxury fashion magazines. By merging
fashion imagery, beauty advice, lifestyle
journalism, and coverage of social events, the
formula of "the glossy" has remained relatively
unchanged since the introduction of the first
regular fashion magazine, *The Lady's Magazine*,
in the 1770s. Titles such as *Vogue*, *Harper's
Bazaar*, *Elle,* and *Marie Claire* have cultivated
their own styles while remaining a cornerstone
of the fashion industry through their highly
commercial approach and close links with
advertisers, who significantly influence the
content of an issue. The function of the glossy,
however, extends beyond that of mere promotion
of the latest trends. Documenting shifts across
contemporary culture, they form an authoritative
filter through which changing ideals of identity,
beauty, and femininity are reflected and
constructed. Their combination of text and
imagery translates trends into a comprehensible
consumer language, suggesting new identities
and validating existing ones. The establishment
of international editions provides a space for
the projection of culture-specific ideals while
reflecting the increasing global reach and
influence of the contemporary fashion industry.

3-MINUTE DETAILING
The advent of the Internet
prompted a decline in the
sales of fashion print
media, with the immediacy
of online formats providing
readers with an accessible
and unedited alternative
source of fashion imagery
and reportage. Luxury
online fashion retailer
Net-a-porter.com,
however, successfully
reversed this trend with
the 2014 launch of a glossy
print magazine *Porter*,
which symbolized a return
of the magazine as a
desirable and aspirational
fashion object in its
own right.

3-SECOND BIOGRAPHIES
CONDÉ MONTROSE NAST
1873–1942
Publisher who founded Condé
Nast Publications in 1909

DIANA VREELAND
1903–89
Influential fashion editor
known as "The Empress of
Fashion"

ANNA WINTOUR
1949–
Editor-in-Chief of American
Vogue since 1988 and Artistic
Director of Condé Nast
Publications since 2013

EXPERT
Julia Rea

*Glossies offer readers
a curated selection
of escapism, fantasy,
spectacle, and aspiration.*

EDITORIAL

An editorial is a series of

photographs commissioned by a magazine that appear together either online or in print. Rather than merely showcasing things for sale, they attempt to capture a mood, feeling, or idea through the use of garments, accessories, and beauty products. Although distinct narratives and even individual garments may be difficult to decipher, they offer a glimpse at a stylized world and wearer for the season's latest clothes. Editorials are collaborative efforts that involve designers, stylists, models, magazine editors, and photographers. The choice of location, assembly of looks and the individuals—both in front of and behind the camera—all shape the resulting images. In a sense, fashion editorials imbue the garments they depict with the mood and ideas the photographs communicate. While a floor-length burgundy wool coat is quite traditional in its construction, when worn by model/actress Tilda Swinton and photographed by Tim Walker, it becomes a futuristic uniform, modern, slick, and *au courant*. By capturing an imagined moment, such as that which the camera fixes in front of its lens, fashion editorials gesture at larger desires, both socially and style-wise, simultaneously tapping into desire and creating demand.

3-SECOND BIOGRAPHIES
RICHARD AVEDON
1923–2004
Noted photographer whose work redefined fashion photography

TIM WALKER
1970–
Prominent photographer whose work has shaped the look of *Vogue* for over a decade

EXPERT
Rebecca Straub

Familiar to anyone who has thumbed through the pages of Vogue, editorials capture and create fashion's photographic fantasies.

ADVERTISING

Fashion advertising has typically consisted of visual representations of garments and accessories. Be they the hand-colored illustrations of the first regular fashion magazines of the late eighteenth century, or controversial Calvin Klein Underwear ads in the 1990s, high-end fashion houses create seasonal advertisements shot by leading photographers and purchase ad space in glossy magazines such as *Vogue* and *Elle*. Both the September and March issues devote a majority of their content to advertising, thus they are important not only for ushering in the look of a new season, but also for ad sales, with clients vying for desirable placement among their pages. Yet, as is the case with the fashions portrayed, advertising is equally subject to the tastes of industries in constant flux. While fashion advertising has historically been tied to magazines, increasingly new forms of media are employed to expand consumer bases and access wider audiences no longer bound by geography or by time. The adoption of digital strategies by fashion advertisers follows with larger market trends. Online advertising expenses in the United States, which include publications, video, search engine keywords, and email marketing, now exceed the $111.5 billion spent on print.

3-SECOND SKETCH
Fashion advertisements often feature actors, models, and other famous faces with the intent to sell the products or projected lifestyles they picture.

3-MINUTE DETAILING
Online advertising does not merely place content on websites. Instead, the most growth has occurred in the realms of social media and network building. In bypassing traditional print-based media, brands reach larger audiences without purchasing ad space. Chanel's Instagram feed boasts 4.9 million followers, far exceeding American *Vogue*, which has a total average circulation of only 1.2 million, including both paid subscriptions and single copy purchasers.

RELATED ENTRIES
See also
THE GLOSSIES
page 120

EDITORIAL
page 122

BLOGS
page 132

3-SECOND BIOGRAPHIES
BRUCE WEBER
1946–
Photographer known for his advertising work for Calvin Klein, Abercrombie & Fitch, and Versace

INEZ VAN LAMSWEERDE & VINOODH MATADIN
1963– & 1961–
Fashion photographers responsible for iconic Dior, Givenchy, and Balenciaga campaigns

EXPERT
Rebecca Straub

Often resulting in images that resemble editorial features, advertising aims to sell the fashions and fragrances it pictures.

STYLE MAGAZINES

3-SECOND SKETCH
Although it is now commonplace to see entire blogs devoted to how people dress, style magazines paved the way for the industry's and consumers' interest in street style.

3-MINUTE DETAILING
Photography played a large role in defining the visual identities of individual style magazines. Notable photographers such as Nick Knight, Corinne Day, Wolfgang Tillmans, and Juergen Teller all created pictures that pushed at the boundaries of what was considered fashion photography. Their raw and seemingly unstaged images of real bodies—acne, bruises, and all—stood in stark contrast to the hourglass figures and perfectly coiffed hair in the pages of *Vogue*.

Though known for glamor

and excess, the 1980s also gave rise to an increasingly visible flip-side of high fashion. Style magazines such as *Arena*, *BLITZ*, *i-D*, and *The Face* combined music, politics, pop culture, and street style, to describe fashion in the world and off the runway. In the wake of punk and other such DIY movements, style magazines created a public platform outside mainstream fashion media. In 1980, Nick Logan started *The Face* to "escape from struggling to explain myself to publishers. . ." Free from such restriction, style magazines attempted to document the look and feel of youth culture as much as the music and fashion on which they reported. *i-D* introduced the "Straight-Up" street portrait, shot outside against a blank wall, which offered a detailed picture of British teens, and traced trends amongst their efforts at self-fashioning. Stylists including Ray Petri, a favorite of both *i-D* and *The Face*, created many of the iconic images associated with style magazines. Using street-cast models, Petri brought diversity to an often whitewashed industry, and androgyny to one built on gender binaries. The look was both assertive and eclectic, and *The Face* was hailed as the UK's newest "style-bible." Magazines that documented fashion trends at the margins were now setting them for the mainstream.

RELATED ENTRIES
See also
ANDROGYNY
page 46

STYLISTS
page 128

STREET PHOTOGRAPHY
page 142

3-SECOND BIOGRAPHIES
TERRY JONES
1945–
Formerly the art director of British *Vogue*, cofounded *i-D* magazine

NICK LOGAN
1947–
Credited with inventing style magazines by launching *The Face* in 1980

CORINNE DAY
1962–2010
Photographer whose subversive take on fashion photographs resulted in some of the first published images of Kate Moss in *The Face* in 1990

EXPERT
Rebecca Straub

Style magazines look beyond mainstream and high fashion to define what's cool.

THE FACE No. 48

96 PAGES   APRIL 1984 80p

THE FACE

IRRESISTIBLE!

INSIDE:
Sade
lets her
hair down

simple
minds
matt
dillon
ian dury
aswad
french
& saunders
bruce weber

STYLE:
the new -
glitterati

SCOOP:
HOW WE HOAXED THE **RED ARMY**

Photo: Jamie Morgan

STYLISTS

3-SECOND SKETCH

Through a closely collaborative relationship, the stylist is instrumental in shaping and articulating the creative vision and constructing the identity of designers, brands, and publications.

3-MINUTE DETAILING

Stylists have the power to cross the boundary into popular culture, creating iconic and enduring fashion imagery. British stylist Melanie Ward, for example, collaborated with photographer Corinne Day on the iconic cover story of *The Face* magazine's July 1990 issue, launching the career of model Kate Moss. Ward blended a barefaced Moss, knitted sweaters, nudity, and feathered headdresses to create a naturalistic series of images that both captured and defined the mood of a generation.

The fashion stylist has become one of the industry's most influential figures, lending their creative vision to the production of fashion shows, magazine editorials, and advertising campaigns. Formerly working solely behind the scenes, the top stylists are now high-profile figures in their own right, each cultivating their own signature style identity and methodology. The notion of collaboration remains central to the work of a stylist, both through the working process itself and through their employment as creative consultants and contributing editors to designers, brands, and publications. Katy England, for example, is renowned for her long-term creative partnership with Alexander McQueen, styling his shows and providing sources of design inspiration that helped to shape his aesthetic. Through their instinctive interpretation and, often, subversion of a brand's creative vision, stylists combine and alter garments, utilize accessories, and coordinate hair and makeup in unexpected and exciting ways, in order to construct a coherent image, injecting an aesthetic with essential narrative. Stylists are increasingly stepping outside the confines of the commercial and pushing the boundaries of fashion imagery by infusing each final image or collection with imagination, fantasy, and, at times, a vital dose of realism.

RELATED ENTRIES

See also
ALEXANDER MCQUEEN
page 26

SHOWS
page 80

EDITORIAL
page 122

ADVERTISING
page 124

3-SECOND BIOGRAPHIES

GRACE CODDINGTON
1941–
British former model and stylist who has been Creative Director at American *Vogue* since 1988

ISABELLA BLOW
1958–2007
Stylist and editor renowned for her extrovert personal style and for nurturing the careers of designer Alexander McQueen and milliner Philip Treacy

EXPERT

Julia Rea

Stylists unite the different elements of an image in order to create a coherent narrative.

1983
Born in London

2006
Studies history at
University College
London

2006
Begins writing the *Style
Bubble* blog using her
childhood nickname,
Susie Bubble

2008
Begins working as
Commissioning Editor
at DazedDigital.com

2010
Leaves her job at
DazedDigital.com to
blog full-time

2010
Appears in advertising
campaign for The Gap

2013
Her blog reaches 214,000
followers

2013
Asked by the Fashion
Museum, Bath to select
Dress of the Year for 2013

SUSIE BUBBLE

The British blogger Susanna Lau, aka Susie Bubble, is widely considered to be one of the most popular fashion bloggers and a veritable fashion celebrity. She was born in London to a family of Hong Kong Chinese origin. After studying history at University College London, she became a journalist and worked as commissioning editor of DazedDigital.com, the online version of *Dazed & Confused* magazine. Lau started her blog, *Style Bubble*, in 2006, and it soon grew to attract thousands of visitors each day. The nickname "Bubble" stems from her early school days and refers to her self-described status as an "outcast" who lives in a world of her own. In 2010, she left her position at DazedDigital to blog full-time.

Style Bubble represents Lau's personal style, her outfit choices, and opinions on fashion events. The blog aims to "spotlight young and unknown talent" as well as established designers and brands. The first photographs she took for the blog were frequently done using the "camera-in-the-mirror" method and were taken on balconies, in living rooms or backyards. Her eclectic style is exuberant and often demonstrates a fun approach. She is a fan of color-blocking and has an eye for detail, preferring striking accessories. Sometimes her choices are eccentric, such as blue stockings hoisted by old-fashioned garter straps, and inevitably attract attention. According to Lau, her "personal staples" are: "Salvatore Ferragamo bow flats, a gray jersey T-shirt that hangs right, a proper pair of black opaque tights, vintage slip dresses/skirts, and some well-fitting leather gloves."

Besides blogging, Lau also works as a freelance fashion journalist. Her texts are normally written in a very light colloquial tone and contain sharp opinions and thoughtful, sometimes sarcastic comments. Lau has collaborated with numerous brands including Dr Martens, Giorgio Armani, Hong Kong boutique Joyce, department store Selfridges, Google Boutiques project, and the Gap 2010 holiday campaign, in which she described her style as "the wrapping paper of my life." The latter two were also the themes of her "advertorial" posts.

In 2013, the Fashion Museum in Bath asked Susie Lau to select the Dress of the Year. She was the first fashion blogger approached for this purpose. Lau chose a pink dress trimmed with white lace and anarchic black gaffer tape by the British designer Christopher Kane, one of the admirers of her blog. This event was a sign of a growing influence of fashion bloggers and new forms of interactions between traditional costume institutions and famous bloggers.

Olga Vainshtein

BLOGS

3-SECOND SKETCH

From their humble amateur beginnings at the birth of user-generated online content, fashion bloggers have become increasingly professional and influential within the industry.

3-MINUTE DETAILING

Fashion blogs are used not only for self-branding, but also for activism. They create spaces of empowerment for people who are traditionally marginalized by the fashion industry and Western-oriented values, such as plus-sized women or people from ethnic minorities.

A fashion blog is an online

journal devoted to fashion and individual outfit choices. The first fashion blogs appeared in the early 2000s and aimed to express the personal style of independent enthusiasts who were not professionally connected with the industry. Up until then, the traditional fashion media—magazines and newspaper columns—were the main channels of information, but with the emergence of Web 2.0. the number of fashion blogs quickly increased. Combining photographs with short texts, sharing the stories of their favorite pieces and their shopping secrets, the authors constructed a unique space for self-presentation, attracting numerous fans. Bloggers interact with their readers and this two-way communication creates a sense of shared values. In recent years, blogs have become increasingly influenced by commerce with sponsored posts and advertising space. The most successful bloggers can become celebrities in their own right, sometimes given seats on the front row at shows. Chiara Ferragni of *The Blonde Salad*, Nicole Warne of *Gary Pepper Girl,* and Zanita Whittington of *Zanita.com.au* appeared on the cover of fashion magazine *Lucky* in 2015. Bloggers have also collaborated with fashion brands, for example Jane Aldridge with Urban Outfitters and Tavi Gevinson with ModCloth.

RELATED ENTRIES

See also
FRONT ROW
page 92

COLLABORATIONS
page 112

SUSIE BUBBLE
page 130

STREET PHOTOGRAPHY
page 142

3-SECOND BIOGRAPHIES

BRYAN YAMBAO
1981–
Author of *Bryanboy*, famous for his signature pose

RUMI NEELY
1983–
Author of *Fashiontoast.com*

CHIARA FERRAGNI
1987–
Author of *The Blonde Salad*

EXPERT
Olga Vainshtein

Blogs offer an alternative, more personal, take on the fashion industry than the mainstream media.

STYLE BUBBLE

SUSIE FAVES

SOCIAL

The New Gucci Girl

Fabric of India

SUSIE FAVES

VIDEO

Mirabilia Romae

In association with L'Officiel Paris and led by the gorgeous actress Diane Kruger (who is also the Tricentenaire Ambassador), Martell reveals the 300 most influential talents (art, fashion, entertainment, gastronomy and mixology) who best represents the French Art de Vivre in the 21st century. Photographer Patrick Demarchelier, fashion designer Joseph Altuzarra and blogger Garance Doré are included in the list.

ZZZZZEEE TYYYYY
UUUUUIII PPPAAAAA
SSSSSDDD GHHHHHH
JJJJJKKK MMMWWWWW
XXXXCCCC BBBNNNN
Sééé ééé qqqqq ((((((

STREET STYLE

b-boy The b is short for break, as in break dancing, which emerged on the streets of New York in the late 1970s and early 1980s. To engage in competitive dancing in the instrumental breaks of dance tracks, the b-boy style needed tracksuits and sneakers to move in and baseball caps to protect the head, a highly influential look that has continued to evolve as rap and hip-hop hit the mainstream.

brogue Originally rough shoes from Scotland and Ireland, brogues are now associated with a country look and are identified by a decorative pattern of perforated leather across the toe and down the side of the shoe.

dandy A man who affects extreme elegance, often in imitation of aristocratic dressing, or shows excessive concern in his clothing and overall appearance. This can be at some personal cost, whether comfort or economic, or both.

Edwardian Referring to the style and fashions of the Edwardian period, 1901–10, and typified by the elegantly tailored suits of King Edward VII and his fashionable wife Alexandra, who personified Edwardian femininity.

gothic An architectural style prevalent in Europe from the twelfth century and characterized by pointed arches. It is typified by medieval cathedrals and churches such as Sainte-Chapelle in Paris. The gothic revival of the mid-eighteenth and early nineteenth centuries encompassed literature and decorative arts too. Now "gothic" also encompasses melodrama, an element of the supernatural, the grotesque, mystery, and dread, typified by dark clothing and makeup.

MC Short for master of ceremonies or mic controller. Essentially the rapper in hip-hop music, the MC is the person who speaks over the beat, either live or on a recording, while the DJ mixes the beat.

Rococo Originally a French architectural style popular around 1730–50, typified by the extravagant use of sinuous curves and scrolls, which became popular in England in the mid-eighteenth century. The word can also mean florid, excessively detailed, and overly elaborate.

social media An umbrella term for internet media that allows users to interact, share, and exchange information, whether text, video, images, or other multimedia, and create social and professional online networks.

street style Fashion innovations or trends that come from, for example, music or subcultural arenas, that is the "street," rather than from fashion designers. These may then influence elite and mainstream fashion, for instance, the black leather motorcycle jacket.

subculture A group that has a strong shared outlook and interests that differ from the majority or mainstream culture and can manifest itself, for example, through a combination of fashion, music, and politics.

TEDDY BOYS & GIRLS

RELATED ENTRIES
See also
MOVIES
page 42

NOSTALGIA
page 50

LONDON
page 56

3-SECOND SKETCH

As the first representatives of British youth culture, Teddy Boys and Girls defined the style of the postwar generation through their rebellious attitude and dress.

3-MINUTE DETAILING

Despite their thoroughly British roots, Teddy Boys and Girls were strongly influenced by the parallel American rock 'n' roll movement and its iconic figures. Movie stars such as James Dean and Marlon Brando epitomized the rule-breaking spirit at the heart of their modern, rebellious style, while musicians including Elvis Presley and Bill Haley provided the soundtrack central to the Teddy Boy and Girl lifestyle. Later Teddy Girls also adopted the full skirts and neck scarves popularized in 1950s America.

Originating in the working class communities of 1950s London, the Teddy Boy subculture emerged in the aftermath of post-war austerity. Deriving their name from an abbreviation of "Edwardian," the Teddy Boy uniform was inspired by the Edwardian dandies of the early twentieth century: tapered pants, velvet collars, long jackets, vests, and narrow ties. Their distinctive style endeavored to reject the conservative dress of the previous generation and differentiate themselves as a new youth demographic whose financial affluence allowed them to indulge in leisure pursuits, such as movies and music, and wear costly garments. Tight "drainpipe" pants that exposed the socks, soft crepe-soled shoes, and grease-sculpted hair constructed a defiant image of rebelliousness. Imbuing traditional notions of femininity with a new assertive quality, Teddy Girls combined draped jackets and flat shoes with either rolled-up jeans or straight pencil skirts as a sartorial accompaniment to their tough attitude and desire for independence. Although restricted by their lower wages and customary domestic roles, Teddy Girls nonetheless formed Britain's first female youth subculture. The contemporary media, however, often sensationalized "the Teds," portraying them as a socially disruptive gang culture.

3-SECOND BIOGRAPHIES

JAMES DEAN
1931–55
Actor whose defiant dress and attitude and 1955 movie *Rebel Without A Cause* influenced the Teddy Boy movement

VIVIENNE WESTWOOD & MALCOLM MCLAREN
1941– & 1946–2010
Design duo whose London boutique temporarily revived the Teddy Boy aesthetic in the 1970s

EXPERT
Julia Rea

Edwardian dandies and American rock 'n' roll music collided in the defiant aesthetic of the Teddy Boys.

Picture Post, 29 May, 1954

THE TRUTH ABOUT
THE 'TEDDY BOYS'
AND THE TEDDY GIRLS

The 'Edwardians,' or 'Teddy Boys,' have been branded as hooligans, juvenile gangsters and delinquents. They have also been called dandies and mother's darlings. It is a confusing picture of exaggeration and distortion. A PICTURE POST investigation seeks to bring it into focus. Our staff writer, HILDE MARCHANT, presents the facts. A PSYCHIATRIST of much experience with young people, interprets them. JOSEPH McKEOWN took the pictures

WE were in a dance-hall in Tottenham—a suburb of London—and the young men we wished to contact were distinctive and obvious. The Boys' jackets hung to their knees, the poplin shirts were advertisement white, the trousers were ankle tight, the shoes were good black leather, and the ties were narrow bows. An ugly outfit? That is a matter of opinion, and we were not seeking opinion—only facts. To approach the facts meant we had first to approach the boys, talk to them, and challenge the honesty of their talk. And the first thing that struck me was that their clothes are deceptive. This Edwardian fashion gives a uniformity to a group of young people who are far from uniform. They are as varied, diverse and informal as any other group of human beings. They set a pattern in their velvet collars, dog-tooth checks and moccasin shoes. But there is no such standard pattern about their lives or behaviour.

But let them talk for themselves, for they are frank enough. What do they do during the days or the week? One is a toy maker, one a glass cutter. Another is an engineer's apprentice, one a die-cutter, another an electric welder and, surprisingly, another a National Serviceman on leave—back in his Teddy Boy civilian 'uniform.' (His hair was shorter than the others, but would still have horrified the Sergeant-major.) Their wages were good—ranging from the £4 12s. 6d. a week apprentice to over £11 a week for the skilled cabinet maker. Their suits cost between £17 and £20. All of them agreed that a good poplin shirt was just under £2 and that a pair of shoes was around the £5 mark. Most of them 'kept themselves', which means they pay their parents something towards the rent and the household budget. Even so, pocket money was never less than £2 a week, and often double. They were not interested in drink—a beer perhaps, but more likely a mineral water. They

THE SUIT THAT GRANDFATHER MIGHT HAVE WORN
The dance is contemporary jive. But the suit is an adaptation of the Edwardian 'masher's' outfit. It is also English in conception and, unlike recent men's fashions, owes nothing to Hollywood.

PUNK

RELATED ENTRIES
See also
VIVIENNE WESTWOOD
page 28

3-SECOND SKETCH
Originally anarchic,
nihilistic, and shocking
but also highly original,
eclectic, and experimental,
punks were unfairly
reduced to a stereotype
by the media of the time.

3-MINUTE DETAILING
Arguably a precursor to
London, the New York
scene was influenced by
musicians such as Lou Reed
and Iggy Pop. McLaren was
also briefly manager of the
seminal New York Dolls
before the formation of the
Sex Pistols and the London
movement took off.
Focused around the CBGB
club in Lower Manhattan,
bands such as the
Ramones, Blondie, the
Patti Smith Group, and
Television both inspired
and drew musical and
visual influences from the
parallel London scene.

Against a background of rising
unemployment and economic stagnation, punk
was a youth movement that emerged in London
and New York in the mid-1970s, as the antithesis
to the hippy movement. The London scene was
channeled by Malcolm McLaren and Vivienne
Westwood, firstly through their boutique SEX,
at the unfashionable end of the King's Road in
Chelsea, which sold innovative clothing made
from materials such as leather and rubber, and
then by the formation of the Sex Pistols in 1975,
who also modeled their clothing and were
managed by McLaren. Aggressive, anarchic, and
perverse, both punk clothing and music set out
to shock the older generation. The do-it-yourself
approach that underpinned and gave strength
to the movement resulted in a highly original
look, with various stylistic inspirations, for
instance, rocker and skinhead influences drawn
together in one look. The customization of
items of clothing with studs, holes, graffiti, and
rips, often repaired with safety pins, created
what were seen at the time as outrageous
garments. Punk is still frequently referenced
by designers, although Westwood herself has
moved on. Perhaps its most important legacy
today, however, is its spirit of anarchic collation,
drawing together unrelated pieces to form an
original look that reflects our personalities.

3-SECOND BIOGRAPHIES
DEBORAH HARRY
1945–
Lead singer and songwriter
in punk and new wave band
Blondie

MALCOLM MCLAREN
1946–2010
Music impresario and one of
the initiators of the punk
movement in London

PATTI SMITH
1946–
Singer/songwriter whose debut
album, *Horses*, released in
1975, was hugely influential

EXPERT
Alison Toplis

Rude and rebellious,
punk clothing
countered the
mainstream and
invited comment.

STREET PHOTOGRAPHY

RELATED ENTRIES
See also
COLLABORATIONS
page 112

BLOGS
page 132

BILL CUNNINGHAM
page 144

3-SECOND SKETCH
Many street style blogs now evolve into lifestyle sites specializing in cool hunting, their authors representing a new breed of traveler, the "blog-trotter."

3-MINUTE DETAILING
Blogs on street style effortlessly transgress the boundaries of the social media format. In 2009, Penguin published a best-selling anthology of *Facehunter* images. Fashion magazines now contain columns on street style. Vogue.co.uk has a section on "street chic"; Style.com includes "Street" with reports from photographer Tommy Ton. Celebrity bloggers collaborate with brands, for example Scott Schuman of *The Sartorialist*, collaborated with Burberry in the advertising project "Art of the Trench."

Many of the most popular street style blogs, such as *The Sartorialist*, *Facehunter*, and *Coolhunter*, feature photographs of real people in urban environments. The aim of their photography shoots is to catch a chance fashion moment that "just happens to be." However, the history of street photography begins much earlier; the pioneers of the genre are considered to be Eugène Atget, Paul Martin, and Henri Cartier-Bresson who produced arresting depictions of everyday life in the city. Professional fashion photographers, such as Richard Avedon, Norman Parkinson, and David Bailey, also did occasional shoots in the street, but mainly with professional models. Bill Cunningham was one of the first street photographers to make the genre recognizable and widely accepted. In street style blogs the goal is to satisfy a public demand for a more democratic view on fashion by showing ordinary people wearing imaginative outfits in daily life. Visual representation involves snapshot aesthetics rather than carefully arranged fashion scenes. People are not posing and sometimes the view is taken from behind. An opposite trend in street photography relies on the "Straight Up" pose, where the subject faces the camera and is seen from "tip to toe." This format was first widely used in the British magazine *i-D* founded by Terry Jones in 1980.

3-SECOND BIOGRAPHIES
SCOTT SCHUMAN
1968–
American blogger and photographer who started *The Sartorialist* blog in 2005

GARANCE DORÉ
1975–
French street style blogger, illustrator, and photographer who started her blog www.garancedore.fr in 2006

YVAN RODIC
1977–
Swiss blogger and journalist who started his street style blog *Facehunter* in 2006

EXPERT
Olga Vainshtein

Street photography is now widely used in mainstream fashion journalism.

1929
Born in Boston,
Massachusetts

1948
Drops out of Harvard
University and moves to
New York where he
begins working at Bonwit
Teller department store

1963
Hired as a writer at
Women's Wear Daily

1978
His first "On The Street"
column appears in the
New York Times

1978
Publishes *Facades*, a
collection of photographs
of Editta Sherman
standing in Manhattan
streets

2008
Awarded the Officier
de l'ordre des Arts et
des Lettres by the French
Ministry of Culture

2010
The documentary film
*Bill Cunningham New
York* debuts in cinemas

2012
Awarded the Carnegie
Hall Medal of Excellence

2016
Dies in New York

BILL CUNNINGHAM

Bill Cunningham was the
unofficial founder of street style photography.
He became a fixture of the New York fashion
scene, riding around the city on a bicycle in his
signature blue coat, camera strapped across his
chest. Long before the internet and social
media made street style photography a global
phenomenon, Bill Cunningham was pioneering
the genre on the pages of the *New York Times*.
His photography spread "On the Street" first
appeared in the *Times* in 1978, and remained a
regular feature of the paper. Unlike other style
photographers of the time, Cunningham's
photographs were not always of the elite and
famous, but rather showed a mixture of
everyday people, socialites, and celebrities.
He said he was more interested in capturing
genuine personal style than in photographing
someone recognizable.

While Cunningham also took photos at
seasonal fashion weeks, and at social events
in a column called "Evening Hours," he was best
known for his glimpses of New York street life.
His street style photographs were characterized
by their candid nature. Cunningham would
often capture these images stealthily,
unbeknown to his subjects, and sometimes
without obtaining their permission to reproduce
the images. Supposedly, his first spread for the
Times came together around an image he had
managed to snap of the ever-elusive movie star
Greta Garbo. In the spreads, Cunningham
collaged his favorite shots together, and often
arranged the images to demonstrate a theme,
trend, or even color. In recent years, Cunningham
also produced video forms of these spreads for
the *New York Times* website.

Interestingly, hats, not photographs, first
drew Cunningham to fashion. Born in Boston,
he moved to New York in 1948, after dropping
out of Harvard. He began working in advertising
at Bonwit Teller department store and also
dabbled in his true passion—millinery (hat
making). After briefly serving in the US Army,
Cunningham returned to New York and took
up millinery again, which got him noticed by
Women's Wear Daily editor John Fairchild, who
asked Cunningham to write for him. Cunningham
also wrote for the *Chicago Tribune* and *Details*
magazine. But in 1966, a friend and colleague
gave him his first camera, telling him to "use
it like a notebook"—and the rest is history.

In 2010, a documentary film was produced
on Cunningham's life. It revealed his eccentric
lifestyle. At that point, he still lived in a tiny
studio apartment in Carnegie Hall Tower filled
almost entirely with file cabinets of his work
and just a small cotlike bed. Cunningham
claimed the majority of his work had never been
published. Some speculate that the cabinets
contained the most comprehensive view of
New York fashion over the last four decades.

Emma McClendon

HIP-HOP

RELATED ENTRIES
See also
SPORT
page 44

NEW YORK
page 60

MENSWEAR
page 104

3-SECOND SKETCH
Like the spin of a record, hip-hop influences fashion and then circles back to see itself as a source of inspiration.

3-MINUTE DETAILING
Hip-hop was born at a block party in New York's South Bronx when an MC first rhymed over a breakbeat to the sound of turntables being scratched. Since 1973, hip-hop has been a cultural movement built by rappers, DJs, b-boys, and graffiti artists. While high fashion looked to capture its likeness and use it to its advantage, entrepreneurial designers such as Harlem's Dapper Dan made innovative high-end counterfeits bringing Gucci and Louis Vuitton to his loyal clientele.

With no singular expression, hip-hop style varies depending on time and artist. Rapper Grandmaster Flash favored leather pants and fringed denim jackets in typical 1970s style. In the late 1980s, Run-D.M.C. popularized tracksuits, gold chains, and Adidas shell toe sneakers. N.W.A., whose music described a grittier urban reality, wore baseball caps and baggy T-shirts emblazoned with the name of their hometown, Compton. From the 1990s onward, artists such as Sean "Puff Daddy" Combs and Ma$e adopted a look that spoke more of luxury and lifestyle, wearing leather suits and chinchilla jackets. Recognizing that fans like to dress like the artists they idolize, Sean Combs and Jay Z parlayed their personal style into the successful sportswear lines Sean John and Rocawear. Luxury brands have influenced hip-hop style—Gucci, Prada, and Versace have all been namechecked in song lyrics—but street style has also trickled up to influence high fashion as many established designers have collaborated and clothed hip-hop's biggest stars. Tommy Hilfiger famously dressed R&B singer Aaliyah in a top shaped like his logo, and Marc Jacobs asked rapper Kanye West to design a sneaker for Louis Vuitton.

3-SECOND BIOGRAPHIES
SHAWN CARTER (JAY Z)
1969–
Rapper, producer, and founder of Rocawear clothing line

SEAN COMBS (PUFF DADDY)
1969–
Rapper, producer, and founder of Sean John clothing line

MISSY ELLIOTT
1971–
Songwriter, rapper, and record producer

KANYE WEST
1977–
Influential producer, rapper, and designer

EXPERT
Rebecca Straub

Hip-hop has set music and fashion trends ever since its inception.

SAPEURS

3-SECOND SKETCH

Often called modern-day dandies, the Sapeur lifestyle involves more than just the appearance of wealth and stylish clothes—for many, it represents freedom of expression despite political subjugation.

3-MINUTE DETAILING

SAPE has been criticized as a rejection of African tradition in favor of colonial style. Yet the Sapeurs embody a sharply tailored vision of pacifist sophistication rooted in the political and economic hardships faced by Central Africans. An intensified international interest in SAPE is evidenced in the 2012 music video "Losing You" by Solange Knowles, as well as the 2014 Guinness ad campaign, both of which featured members of SAPE, farther spreading their image abroad.

Hailing from Central Africa, Les Sapeurs take their name from the acronym SAPE, meaning Société des Ambianceurs et des Personnes Élégantes. With an attention to menswear details and a taste for tailored suits, Sapeurs wear brightly colored jackets, bowler hats, and brogues. These Congolese men dress in the regalia of European wealth, yet hail from countries—the Democratic Republic of the Congo and the Republic of the Congo—where nearly half of citizens live at or below the national poverty line. The most widely reported origin story cites the advent of SAPE at the end of Belgian and French colonial rule in 1960, when the capitals of Kinshasa and Brazzaville became cosmopolitan centers on opposing sides of the Congo River. Affluent Africans returned from travel with clothing fresh from Europe, creating a taste among the Congolese for Occidental finery. However, when Joseph Mobutu took power and renamed the country Zaire, he implemented a non-Western dress code. In response, Papa Wemba of the popular musical group Viva La Musica began dressing in three-piece suits and polished leather shoes, with many Congolese fans following suit.

RELATED ENTRIES

See also
SAVILE ROW
page 100

MENSWEAR
page 104

3-SECOND BIOGRAPHY

PAPA WEMBA
1949–
Singer of Viva La Musica, credited with popularizing the Sapeur look

EXPERT

Rebecca Straub

Dressed in polished suits and politically active, the Sapeurs are known for their statement-making sartorial decisions.

LOLITAS

Lolita fashion is a form of

Japanese street style that emerged in the late 1980s. Often dismissed as little more than doll-like makeup, ruffles, and lace, it began as a reaction to sexualized representations of women in Japanese culture. It displays an almost confrontational femininity that prizes elegance and modesty over seduction. Lolita fashion can be further categorized by the places from which its wearers draw inspiration. "Sweet Lolita" is the most familiar and oldest form, whose references to *Alice in Wonderland*—knee-length full skirts, pinafores, and a pastel color palette—characterize the look. "Gothic Lolitas" wear black, burgundy, and white, with garments whose shape and construction reference Victorian corsetry. "Punk Lolitas" employ similar colors to their gothic counterparts, but often as part of a tartan or plaid. Present are the familiar trappings of British punk with safety pins, spikes, and bondage straps appearing frequently in wearers' outfits. Japanese Lolitas play with traditional forms of dress, referencing samurai armor and wearing kimonos cropped to showcase stockinged legs. Lolita fashion has grown in popularity outside Japan, including the USA, Europe, and South America, where practitioners often make their own clothes, since few stores cater specifically to Lolita sensibilities.

3-SECOND SKETCH
Those dedicated to Lolita fashion often describe it as a lifestyle that extends beyond the mere act of dressing and involves "living beautifully."

3-MINUTE DETAILING
Many Japanese clothing companies have defined the look of Lolita fashion. The most famous among them, Baby, The Stars Shine Bright, opened in Tokyo in 1988, and offers Sweet Lolita shoppers "light colors and designs inspired by the Rococo era." Although the flagship store is in Japan, the brand has expanded to include an American store in Manhattan.

RELATED ENTRIES
See also
TOKYO
page 66

PUNK
page 140

STREET PHOTOGRAPHY
page 142

EXPERT
Rebecca Straub

Originally a form of Japanese street style, Lolita fashion now has fans and followers across the world.

APPENDICES

RESOURCES

BOOKS

Adorned in Dreams: Fashion and Modernity
Elizabeth Wilson
(I.B. Tauris, 2003)

Alexander McQueen
Claire Wilcox (ed.)
(V&A Publishing, 2015)

*Birds of Paradise: Costume
As Cinematic Spectacle*
Marketa Uhlirova, ed.
(Köenig Books, 2014)

Blitz: As Seen in Blitz: Fashioning '80s Style
Iain R. Webb
(ACC Editions, 2013)

Chanel: The Vocabulary of Style
Jérôme Gautier
(Thames & Hudson, 2011)

The Culture of Fashion
Christopher Breward
(Manchester University Press, 1995)

*Elegance in an Age of Crisis:
Fashions of the 1930s*
Patricia Mears and G. Bruce Boyer (eds.)
(Yale University Press and Fashion Institute
of Technology, 2014)

*The Empire of Fashion:
Dressing Modern Democracy*
Gilles Lipovetsky
(Princeton University Press, 2002)

Fashion
Christopher Breward
(Oxford University Press, 2003)

*Fashion: A History from the 18th Century
to the 20th Century*
Akiki Fukai
(Taschen, 2006)

Fashion at the Edge
Caroline Evans
(Yale University Press, 2003)

Fashion: A Very Short Introduction
Rebecca Arnold
(Oxford University Press, 2009)

*The Fashion History Reader:
Global Perspectives*
Giorgio Riello and Peter McNeil (eds.)
(Routledge, 2010)

Fashion Since 1900
Valerie Mendes and Amy de la Haye
(Thames & Hudson, 2010)

Fashioning the City: Paris, Fashion and the Media
Agnes Rocamora
(I.B. Tauris, 2009)

Fifty Years of Fashion: New Look to Now
Valerie Steele
(Yale University Press, 1997)

The Glass of Fashion
Cecil Beaton
(Rizzoli Ex Libris, 2014)

The Mechanical Smile: Modernism and the First Fashion Shows in France and America, 1900–29
Caroline Evans
(Yale University Press, 2013)

Seeing Through Clothes
Anne Hollander
(University of California Press, 1993)

Street Style
Ted Polhemus
(PYMCA, 2010)

V&A Gallery of Fashion
Claire Wilcox and Jenny Lister
(V&A Publishing, 2013)

WEBSITES

A useful resource for seeing twentieth-century fashions in motion
britishpathe.com

The Museum at the Fashion Institute of Technology, New York
fashionmuseum.fitnyc.edu

The fashion collection of the Metropolitan Museum of Art, New York
metmuseum.org/research/digital-collections/costume-institute

Video channel with daily updates on aspects of fashion, art, and design
nowness.com

Fashion photographer Nick Knight's website provides an expansive view of fashion and visual culture
showstudio.com

The fashion collection of the V&A Museum, London
vam.ac.uk/page/f/fashion

Online home of *Vogue* magazine
vogue.com

NOTES ON CONTRIBUTORS

EDITOR

Rebecca Arnold is Oak Foundation Lecturer in History of Dress and Textiles at The Courtauld Institute of Art in London. She has lectured internationally on contemporary and twentieth-century fashion and her publications include *Fashion: A Very Short Introduction* (OUP, 2009), *The American Look: Fashion, Sportswear & Images of Women in 1930s & 1940s New York* (I.B. Tauris, 2009), and *Fashion, Desire & Anxiety: Image & Morality in the 20th Century* (I.B. Tauris, 2001).

CONTRIBUTORS

Emma McClendon is the Assistant Curator of Costume at The Museum at the Fashion Institute of Technology (FIT) in New York. She holds an MA in the History of Dress from The Courtauld Institute of Art and an MA Honours in Art History from the University of St. Andrews. During her time at The Museum at FIT, she has curated the exhibition *Denim: Fashion's Frontier* (2015) and cocurated *Fashion and Technology* (2012), *Trend-ology* (2013), and *Yves Saint Laurent + Halston: Fashioning the 70s* (2015). Recent publications include the catalog for *Denim: Fashion's Frontier*, as well as her essays on Yves Saint Laurent for the book that accompanied the exhibition *Yves Saint Laurent + Halston*. Her research focuses on twentieth-century fashion with a particular interest in the socio-political implications of clothing and the intersection between fashion and technology. Past publications include "The Political Power of the Online Shop" in *From Production to Consumption: The Cultural Industry of Fashion* (2013), as well as "First Paris Fashions Out of The Sky: The Impact of the 1962 Telstar Satellite on the Transatlantic Fashion System," which appeared in *Fashion Theory* (June, 2014).

Katerina Pantelides is a researcher in dress and dance history and a freelance writer. She completed a PhD entitled "Russian Emigré Ballet and the Body: Paris and New York c.1920–50" at The Courtauld Institute of Art, where she now teaches as a Visiting Lecturer. Katerina has written articles on the intersection of dance, dress, and body culture. She is also a cofounder of Fashion Research Network, an organization that promotes the work of early career scholars in fashion and dress and seeks to unite academic researchers with fashion practitioners and curators.

Julia Rea is a fashion historian and writer. After completing an MA in English Literature at the University of St. Andrews, she received an MA in History of Dress at The Courtauld Institute of Art, where she specialized in modernity, film, and image in America and Europe between 1920 and 1945. She has written on a range of topics including the life and work of Coco Chanel, the history of fashion modeling, costume design in the 2013 movie *The Great Gatsby,* and the changing role and significance of mannequins. She has contributed several essays to the Bloomsbury Fashion Photography Archive, an online resource produced in association with Berg Fashion Library, and has written articles for publications including *Sorbet* magazine.

Rebecca Straub is a graduate student at Yale University in the Department of the History of Art. Previously, she studied garment design and construction at the School of the Art Institute of Chicago. Her research interests include the intersecting material histories of dress and the images that document it.

Alison Toplis is an Honorary Research Fellow at the University of Wolverhampton. She worked for several years as a dress and textiles specialist at Christie's Auctioneers before completing her doctorate in the area of nineteenth-century working-class dress. She has since taught at Central Saint Martins, University of the Arts, London, and lectured and published widely, including her book *The Clothing Trade in Provincial England 1800–1850* (2011). She is also a regular contributor to *Who Do You Think You Are?* magazine.

Olga Vainshtein is a Senior Researcher in the Institute for Advanced Studies in the Humanities at the Russian State University for the Humanities in Moscow. She has taught Fashion Studies in Moscow and was a Visiting Professor at the University of Michigan and Stockholm University. She is the founder of the Russian version of *Fashion Theory* journal and the editor of the book series *Library of Fashion Theory.* Her published works include *Dandy: Fashion, Literature, Lifestyle* and articles such as "Mapping Moscow Fashion," "Russian Dandyism," and "Female Fashion, Soviet Style."

INDEX